KHOMEINI AND ISRAEL

Behrouz Souresrafil

Published 1988

Reprinted in the United States

ABOUT THE AUTHOR

Behrouz Souresafil is an Iranian journalist and writer. He was formerly the editor of the influential Tehran daily *Ayandegan*. He is a respected commentator on Middle Eastern politics, and currently a resident columnist on the weekly *Kayhan* in London.

Gift Presented to
The
Chicago Public Library
C
P
L

CONTENTS

PREFACE

Long before Ayatollah Ruhollah Khomeini and his followers came to power in Iran, they had already set in motion their Islamic ideology and a powerful propaganda campaign against the spread of Jewish influence and especially "zionism" in the region and the world.

In his writings and verbal statements, Khomeini repeatedly called for the annihilation of Israel, obliteration of the zionist movement and the continuous struggle against the "Jews" with the belief that Israel was destroying Islam.

Thus during his exile Khomeini supported all struggles against Israel throughout the world and forged relationships with Palestinian groups, from left to right and from Islamic to Marxist. The Ayatollah accused the Shah of allowing Israel an open hand in Islamic Iran, having military and security ties with Israel, buying arms from the "zionists" and selling them oil. The relationship between Iran and Israel was an important issue during Khomeini's propaganda struggle against the Shah.

Following the success of the Islamic Revolution, strong emphasis was placed on transforming Iran into a fully Islamic society cutting off ties with Israel including economic, political and social exchanges (in line with action against the United States and South Africa).

At that time, while leaders of the Revolution had not yet called for breaking ties with America, they branded Israel the enemy and propagated its annhilation. The Israeli office in Tehran was the first foreign diplomatic mission to be occupied with a lot of fanfare.

Ever since then this apparent policy of the struggle against Israel and zionism by the Islamic Republic has not only undergone no change but in fact each day the leaders of the regime have stepped up their propaganda campaign against Israel in pursuit of their goal of freeing Palestine.

The declaration of World Qods Day, slogans such as "The Way to Jerusalem Is Through Karbala" in its war with Iraq, the demand for the expulsion of Israel from the United Nations, even branding Iraq as zionist and several of their politicians as Jews along with politicians from other countries (like France) are but examples of the Islamic regime's rhetoric.

However, behind all the propaganda and demogoguery lies another reality. The Khomeini regime faced mammoth problems in running the country from the beginning and in a bid to survive turned to Israel. After the occupation of the American Embassy in Tehran and faced with the problems of providing the masses with consumer goods and its own need for military supplies, the Islamic regime tilted towards Israel and of course was welcomed with open arms by that country.

The Iran-Iraq war provided such an impetus to this hitherto secret relationship that it soon gave way to an open door policy, without any cover-ups, and led to military and political cooperation between Jersalem and Tehran. Even Israeli officials confirmed publicly on several occasions that they had forged close ties with the Khomeini regime because of the advantages they derived from such cooperation and even benefitted from a strong Islamic Republic.

Nevertheless, the so called Islamic Republic continued to deny any links between Islamic Iran and zionist Israel and either cancelled or paid no heed to undeniable evidence and documents relating to military and economic cooperation and even exchange of information between the two countries.

However, existing evidence and an unbiased and realistic analysis shows that the Khomeini regime, by weakening the unity of Islamic nations, being instrumental in widening the differences among these nations, prolonging the Iran-Iraq war and numerous other conspiracies in destabilizing the Islamic regimes of the region, not only has undeniable links with Israel but also in practice conforms to the political and military objectives of that country.

The purpose of writing this book is to lend credence to the fact that the so called Islamic Republic, despite all its propaganda and political pronouncements, has a very close and common relationship with Israel and one cannot truly believe that its call for the annihilation of Israel or strike against zionism is genuine.

Simply, the continued existence of the Khomeini regime not only threatens the enemies of Israel and those who oppose it but also provides Israel adequate grounds to the avail of politics and propaganda to confront suggested solutions to the Palestinian problems and other regional and international problems (including peace with the Arabs and determining the fate of the occupied Arab regions).

This book will endeavor to prove its point through presentation of reliable documents, references, writings and undisputable quotations pertaining to the Khomeini regime's contacts, and Ayatollah Khomeini's approval, and at the same time pinpoint the benefits Israel has reaped from the success of the so called Islamic Revolution and the approximately 10 years of clergy rule in Iran.

We will attempt to show differing views on subjects and documents related to the Islamic Republic within the framework of the above discussions in such a manner so that the reader will comprehend the reality of the magnitude of this relationship and be convinced that no basis exists whatsoever for the Tehran regime's propaganda policy and its internal and international propaganda turmoil towards its struggle against zionism and Israel. The book will also show the detrimental factors in this region, international relations and security of the Western and Islamic world.

Until now a complete and detailed analysis of these aspects has not been presented for public opinion and general awareness outside specialized information and political circles.

were deported by Nebuchadazer in 586 and 597 BC after conquest of Judah and who were taken as prisoners and slaves to Babylonia—can not be interpreted as a special love of him for them, rather it should be considered as part of his general governmental policy based on which he gave all nations under his rule complete freedom to keep and observe their religious and cultural traditions. As an example, after conquest of Babylonia, he not only did not interfere with the Babylonian Traditions but, on the contrary, observed the rituals of the Babylonian gods in their Temples. Nevertheless, Cyrus' tolerance and love for freedom which was continued during the reign of most other Achamenid Kings too, created so much affection and love for him in the hearts of the Jews that the name "Cyrus" and all its different versions and forms of pronunciations such as Kurush, Kurus, Chiro, Ciro, etc. is one of the most popular and beloved names that Jews still use to name their children all over the world.

In that respect an incident cited by one of the high ranking officials involved in the Ceremonies for the 2500th Anniversary of the Persian Empire is worth mentioning: "The central office for these ceremonies in Tehran, which were observed in 1971, asked all persons named Cyrus in the world to send their names and addresses to this office so that an album commemorating these ceremonies could be sent to them. The total number of letters received exceeded 30,000."

The Jews' affection for Cyrus was carried to such an extent that during the coming years and centuries after him, several myths concerning his relation and services to the Jewish Nation were created. One such myth is that Cyrus had a Jewish wife who persuaded him to free the Jewish captives in Babylonia. Of course, there is no historical proof to the authenticity of this myth. Another example is the story of "Esther" in which the Jewish myth creators have tried to create a Jewish origin for an Achamenid Queen. According to the story in the "Book of Esther," which was probably compiled after the Achamenids, "Esther", a Jew, was one of the wives of Xerxes. This Jewish Queen not only rescued her nation from a massacre conspired by a minister called Haman but also obtained a decree from Xerxes according to which the Jews were allowed to kill 75,000 of Haman's co-conspirators. It is in commemoration of this incident and the killing of the enemies of the Jews that on the 14th day of Aazar a new celebration-festivity was established called Pourim or Boury which according to Aboo Raihan Albirouni's account in "Athar-al-Baghieh" was also called "the feast of burning Haman."

Cyrus's policy of tolerance and liberalism was continued by his son Kambozia. After conquest of Egypt, he treated the Jewish settlers and their temples with respect. Other Achamenid Kings such as Daryush the Great, Xerxes, Artaxerxes, and Daryush II—though on some occasions they had to abandon Cyrus' policy of liberalism and tolerance due to the rebellions and unrests in their vast empire—but as a whole they generally treated Jews with such respect and tolerance that according to historical and archealogical evidences and Jewish writers and scholars, both, the Achamenid period has been considered one of the periods in which the Jews enjoyed freedom and welfare. The story of Esther and Mordecai, according to which a number of Jews rose to high ranks in Xerxes's Court, is another example of this favorable view of the Jewish historians and storywriters towards Achamenids.

Although, after the downfall of Achamenids, and during the period of their successors—the Parts and Sassanids—due to the strengthening of Zoroasterianism and the influence of the Magis (the Zoroasterian Clergy), the Jews have faced periods of fanatic prosecution and torment in the vast Persian Empire, but according to the majority of Jewish and Non-Jewish historians, the Jews always enjoyed freedom in their life, work and business and had their own temples and their own schools in major cities up until the emergence of Islam and the downfall of Sassanids during the reign of Yazdegerd III. During these long periods coexistence and intermingling among Iranians and Jews, caused interaction and influence between the two cultures, and their social and religious traditions. Several Zoroasterian concepts such as belief in Angles, Satan, Resurrection and "Chinodil" (the bridge to heaven only passable by the righteous) found their way to Judaism and from there to Christianity. This religious and cultural closeness was due to the fact that the two nations, Iranians and Jews, were the only monotheists of the Ancient world before Christ.

With the emergence of Islam and offensive of Moslem Arab Armies against Iran, the last Sassanid King was defeated in 642 AD and Iran lost its independence and became part of the Islamic Empire whose capital was first Damascus and then Baghdad. As a result, the Zoroasterian Religion which was the official religion of the country up until then, was replaced by Islam and all foundations of the Iranian society were deeply altered.

The first collision and struggle between the two cultures and religions of Islam and Judaism date back to the period before conquest of Iran by Arabs. The disputes of Moslems with "the denouncers of Islam," in fact, started during the life of the Prophet himself. According to Quran, on occasions, the Jews and Mohammad himself would debate in the presence of the Prophet, and Mohammad himself would join in some of these debates "ALE EMRAN SURAH". But little by little and as the Islamic government's power increased, these debates and oral disagreements evolved into a relation between the conquerer and the conquered and the Moslem rulers **who evidently did not have a favorable view towards Non Moslem minorities, started using different excuses to oppress and torment them.**

The Zoroasterians, Jews and Christians who did not convert to Islam, were allowed to practice their religions. Living under the Islamic Empire's rules, they were exempted from serving in the armed forces, and from paying the Zakat which is prescribed to Muslims and amount to five percent of a Muslim's holdings. Nevertheless, up until long times after the entry of Arabs and Islamics Muslims into Iran, the Jews who lived there remained and continued their long standing association with the local population, many of whom did not convert to Islam. As an example, Isfahan was, for a period even after the coming of Islam to Iran, called Judah.

In 630 AD, the Arabs were politically unified under Mohammad-the prophet of Islam's leadership. The new government's heads and rulers were from the Aristocracy of Makkah, the Northern and Southern Arabia Tribal chiefs and Prophet's disciples. His successors were called "Khaliphs" and were both the spiritual leader (Imam) and the political ruler. The four Khaliphs, i.e. Aboobakr (who ruled from 634-636), Omar (who ruled from 636-646), Othman (who ruled from 646-658), and Ali (who ruled from 658-663) were all relatives or close disciples of the Prophet.

For the first time, during the rule of Omar, economic and social pressures and regulations coordinating the relationship between Muslims and Non-Muslims, called Dhimmis, were established. Non-Muslims were allowed to worship freely, were exempt from service in the armed forces, were allowed to own property, were permitted to trade and practice their professions. In return, they were obliged not to disrespect the Quran or the Prophet Muhammad. They were prohibited from assaulting Muslim women and from converting Muslims and from helping the enemies of Islam. Such liberal treatment of people of other religions had not been practiced since the time of Cyrus.

One of the significant Jewish figures of the Mongol period was the famous physician "Rashid-ad-Din" whose fame as a historian and politician surpassed most boundaries. One of the Mongol historians writes about this great figure: "He was one of the greatest men that East has produced". From this date onwards, the Jews were employed in courts or governments on and off up to and until the period of Pahlavi Dynasty.

A history of liberalism and oppression towards Non-Muslims followed the decrees of Omar until the establishment of the Safavid Dynasty in Iran in 1502. But from the Safavid period onwards, because Shiism was adopted as the official religion of the country, the discrimination between the Dhimmi and the true believer was intensified as well as between the Sunni Muslim and the Shiism. Specially that from this period onwards, the Moslem religious writers as well as some Jews who had converted to Islam, wrote a host of books in rebuttal of Judaism. The important difference between Jews and Moslems, in addition to religious competition, was in some basic principles. Several Moslem writers believed that Jews have altered the Old Testament and what they have in their hands is not authentic and has a lot of flaws in it; as Ebn Hasm for example, has cited 57 different flaws in the Old Testament. On the other hand, the Jews in defending their religion, cavilled on Islam too. For example, they considered the miracles attributed to Mohammad and believed in by Moslems contrary to the explicit text of Quran in which the performance of miracles by Mohammad is evaded. Some of the Jewish writers and scholars have even doubted Quran as Mohammad's miracle by arguing that even if this claim is true, this miracle cannot convince those Arabs and non Arabs who do not understand the rhetorical eloquence and literary excellence of Quran. They argue: what kind of a Prophet is this whose miracle is only understandable by a small group?

The oppression and prosecution of Jews according to Shiia Laws concerning "uncleanliness" of all non Moslems continued until the eighteenth century, especially during the last decades of Safavid Dynasty, in which the Shiia Clergy, without much success, tried to convert non-Moslems to Islam.

With emergence of Nader Shah (1736-1747), the Jews of Iran found a new savior and were rescued from the prosecution and discrimination of Safavid Period. Nadar Shah abolished Shism as the official religion of the country, showed great tolerance towards non-Moslems, and even invited the Jews to come and settle in Mashad, the holy city of Iranian Shiites.

During the reign of Qajar Kings (1794-1925), and due to the increase of Shiite Clergy's influence, the oppression and torment of Jews was once again restarted. During the period the Clergy provoked the mob rather than the king and as such they caused extreme injustice and killing of Jews. The propaganda and rebellions against

Babism and Bhaism, created and stirred rumors about Jews. Rumors that Jews kill Moslem children and extract their blood to use in their religious rituals are examples of some of the actions of the fanatics against Jews. There are abundant pointers to show that the big merchants and businessmen of bazaar who always considered Jews their tough competitors helped these provocations. In the letters from the Iranian Jews dated July 1897, preserved in the Archives of A.I.U. in Paris, an incident related to this issue in Hamadan, is cited:

"Following the decree that the Shah (Mozaffar-ad-Din Shah) issued 15 days ago in favor of the Jews, the anger and animosity of the Clergy was intensified. For example, in Hamadan, in which there live a big community of Jews, they distributed pamphlets in Mosques asking their followers to kill all the Jews on the 10th of Moharram. The Jews temporarily extinguished the anger of their enemies by dividing 3000 Gharans (1500 Francs) among the Clergy. In Kermanshah, our fellow Jews were not worried as much. They stayed home during the full three day period of the great mornings of Moharram. The Shiite fanaticism was satisfied by killing a few Sunnis."

What helped the Jews of Iran during the Qajar period was the expansion of relations between Iran and Europe, the increase in the influence of the foreign embassies in Iran (especially the British) and the journeys of the Qajar Kings-Nasser ad-Din and Mozaffar-ad-Din Shah to Europe. They wanted to present a civilized and modern picture of themselves and their country to the Europeans.

In 1873, during the official trip of the king of Iran to Europe, the local chapter of "World Jewish Society" in European capitals met with the king and presented to him a list requesting betterment of conditions for Jews in Iran. These requests were repeated in other trips too. Besides, the British Embassy asked Mozaffar-ad-Din Shah to seriously take the Iranian Jews under his protection. The 1897 proclamation of Mozaffar-ad-Din Shah concerning Jews was due to the aforementioned factors:

"In order for all nations, who are His Majesty's obedient subjects, to be able to live in peaceful coexistence, the Moslems have been ordered to stop prosecution and tormenting Jews and forcing them to wear identifying signs. Those who shall commit any action against our non Moslem subjects or shall want to establish a differentiating sign between them and others will be severely punished. All vassals are responsible to distribute this decree issued by His Majesty so that everyone will act according to their rights. Be it that every one obeys His Majesty's wishes with intent."

Although thousands of Iranian Jews, despite all the difficulties caused by Shiite local authorities for them, migrated to Palestine during the 19th century, the Qajar period ended with a relatively nice memory for Iranian Jews because at the time when the constitution for the Constitutional Monarchy was being drafted, the Jewish minority's rights were recognized and they were given the right to vote for and to choose their own representatives in the Parliment.

During the Pahlavi period, oppression and injustice towards Jews decreased to a great extent and the Iranian Jewish community reached a level of freedom, welfare, and wealth relative to its efforts. Twenty years after the establishment of Constitutional Monarchy, Reza Shah Pahlavi (almost concurrent with Mostafa Kamal in Turkey) crashed the huge power of the Shi'a Clergy and started some important reforms and renovations in the basic institutions of the country. He abolished the discrimination and injustice against all minorities. His son Mohammad Rezah Shah followed this policy in earnest and continued it until February 1979 when the Shiite groups led by Ayatollah Ruhallah Khomeini, the leader of Shi'a Clergy, seized power in Iran.

The Iranian Jews mostly remained loyal to the country and the Shah. The Jewish community in Tehran, on the occasion of Mohammad Reza Shah's coronation ordered a special tribute to him to be prepared in Paris. On this tablet which was made of 50 kilograms of gold, ornamented with diamonds and inlayed with rubies, some oracles by "Ezekiel," Cyrus' Cylinder of human rights, and the principles of Shah's White Revolution were inscribed.

Of course, the efforts of Pahlavi Kings to abolish the religious discriminations and reinstitute the rights of the Iranian minorities, including the Jews, was costly for them. The Shi'a Clergy had challenged him from the start of Rezah Shah's rise to power, because of his antifanatic reform programs. In this struggle, which lasted more than 50 years, the Clergy always reprimanded him and his son for these acts and on occasions even accused them of "having sold the country to the Jews and Zionists."

These accusations and other problems rose to new dimensions from 1948, when Iran recognized the newly established State of Israel, which was fully accepted in the United Nations, on a de facto basis.

1. “Israel”. Politique Internationale, No 19, Printemps 1983, p. 92
2. Zarinkoob, Abdulhussein. *No East, No West-But Humaine,* Tehran, Amirkabir, 1356 (Second edition), p. 13
3. Moscati, Sabatino. *The Face of the Ancient Orient,* New York, 1962, p. 288
4. “Shifa, Shoja ad-Din. *Crime and Punishment,* (Iran: 1357-1365 , 4 vols. Paris, Iranshaher Publicaion, 1365 (Vol. III, p. 1686)
5. Ibid, Vol. III, p. 1687
6. “Ibn-Ebree. *The Concise History of Governments,* Beirut, 1980, pp. 81-82
7. “Zarinkoob, Abdulhussein. *No East, No West-But Humaine,* Tehran, Amirkabir, 1356 (Second edition), p. 22
8. *Ibid,* p. 65
9. “Shifa, Shoja ad-Din. *Crime and Punishment,* (the prior resource), Vol. III, p. 1687
10. *Ibid,* p. 1687
11. “Ravandi, Morteza. *The Social History of Iran,* Tehran, Amirkabir, 1356 (Second edition), Vol. II, pp. 61-62.
12. *Ibid,* Vol. II, p. 239
13. “Littman, David. “Les juifs en Perse avant les Pahlavi”, Les Temps Modernes, No. 395, Juin 1979, p. 1913
14. “Pahlavan, Christian. “De l’Amour la Haine”, p. 93
15. “Zarinkoob, Abdulhussein. *No East, No West-But Humaine,* Tehran, Amirkabir, 1356, (Second edition), pp. 95-96
16. “Littman, David, “Les Juifs en Perse avant les Pahlavi”, Les Temps Modernes, No. 395, Juin 1979, p. 1914.
17. *Ibid,* p. 1928
18. *Ibid,* p. 1917
19. *Ibid,* p. 1936
20. “Pahlavan, Christian, “De l’Amour la Haine”, p. 93
21. “Zarinkoob, Abdulhussein, *No East, No West-But Humaine,* Amirkabir, (Second ed.) p. 13.

2

ISRAEL IRAN RELATIONS AND HISTORY

Khomeini's attitude toward Jews, Israel, Zionism, prior to the Revolution:

Ayatollah Khomeini and his regime from moment they took power in 1979, called fighting with Israel (called the occupier of "Qods," Jerusalem) and Zionism one of the major principles of Islamic ideology. The bulk of the oral propaganda and speeches as well as Khomeini's writings and those of his supporters, have continually repeated this theme. That is to say, Zionism is the enemy of humanity, Israel must be destroyed, and that the Jews want to eradicate Islam and dominate the world. One of the the most important slogans of the Islamic Republic throughout its war with Iraq has been "After the taking of Karbala, (the holy city of the Shiites) it will be the turn of Jerusalem." Although the essence of anti-Semitism can be found in the propaganda of Khomeini's Republic and the statements of its top officials, the diplomats of the Islamic Republic abroad have been at pains to tone this down. This anti-Semitic feeling is also hidden by the supposedly **political** struggle against Israel and Zionism.

In the period of radical struggle of Khomeini against the Shah between 1977-78, one of the major accusations made against the Shah was that Iran as been sold to Israel and was now dependent on its supporters, (i.e. the United States). But the conflict between Ayatollah Khomeini and his supporters with Jews and Israel has far deeper roots. In order to understand the ideology of anti-Semitism in the Khomeini Republic, it is necessary to delve back into history.

In 1948, the territory of Palestine, which had become a mandate of the British empire after the first World War, was partitioned by the United Nations into Israel and Palestine; thus realizing what Zionists had worked so hard to achieve since the Balfour declaration in 1917, in which the British foreign secretary promised to establish a Jewish home in Palestine even before Palestine came under British control. Naturally, the Arabs objected. They said that the Palestinian people had not been consulted and rose in protest and the war between the Arabs and Israel started. In this war, although the total population of Arab countries was more than Israel, inter-Arab division and lack of unity coupled with the technical and military superiority of the Jews lead to an Israeli victory. Under the supervision of the United Nations a cessation of hostilities was declared but unofficially a true peace was never found.

From 1948 Israel was accepted into the United Nations as an independent nation, but the state of Iran, as an Islamic nation and out of respect for the position of the Arabs, was not ready to accept Israel. Instead of giving Israel de jure recognition, Iran only accorded her de factor recognition. However, other Moslem nations, such as Turkey, did recognize Israel in full.

There were enough reasons for the monarchical state of Iran to recognize Israel. First, the conflicts were between Israel and Arab countries, because they knew Palestine as an Arab country, but Iran is not an Arab country. Secondly, Iran did not share a border with Israel, and thirdly, Iran really had no conflict of interest with Israel. In addition, the existence of a large Jewish minority in Tehran, many of whom immigrated to the new state of Israel, meant that good relations could readily exist between the two.

Iranian Jewish migration to Palestine had started seriously in the 19th century when thousands of Jews had gone to Palestine and built their lives there. Richard Cottam in his book "Nationalism in Iran" wrote that some of the Jews in the south of Iran emigrated to Jerusalem at the beginning of the Constitutional Revolution. Statistics published in 1960 by the Jewish Information Service showed that prior to that date a total of 47,000 Iranian Jews had left Iran for Israel.

Some Iranian writers, who wished to gain support from the Jewish congressmen and politicans in the United States toward the Shah and his government policies, tried to show that the interests of the Iranian government lay in having good relations with Israel. In any case, there was no logical reason for Iran not to recognize Israel, except the hostile feelings of the Arabs toward Israel, yet the Arabs historically and politically have not been great friends of Iran either. The opposition of the Shiite clergy to Jews for many centuries was based on their belief, which was shared by Iranian merchants and bazaaris, that the establishment of a Jewish state meant empowering Jews who were not only irreligious Kafirs, but also exceptionally good merchants.

Although the Shiite clergy had their own logic for opposing Israel, their solidarity with other Moslem countries meant that many of their reactions to Israel and the problem of Palestine had a different basis. Even before the establishment of the Israeli state, during the period after Reza Shah was removed by the British and the country was occupied by allied forces, the Iranian clergy slowly gained power and began to propagandize against the Jewish state and Iranian Jews on a a large scale. The leadership of this anti-Semitism was in the hand of Seyyed Abol-Ghassem Kashani who was arrested by the English during the Second World War as a (Nazi) fifth columnist and was exiled to Palestine for a time. Kashani, who was extremely ambitious made the struggle against Israel and Jews a religious duty to gain more popularity for organizing supporters around himself.

Kashani's supporters in the south of Tehran plastered up posters which exhorted Iranians to support the Arab Palestinians, to oppose the Israeli state, and made threats against Iranian Jews. In various leaflets they asked people to boycott goods from Jewish merchants and to voluntarily join the Arab militias to go to Palestine to fight the Jews. They also demanded the expulsion of the "Jewish non-Iranians," and warned that if the war between Arabs and Jews were concerned about the repercussions of the Palestine problems inside Iran, no killing would happen; one responsible official said that the government would never allow the Iranian population to kill each other on the basis of such groundless propaganda.

In certain newspapers articles provoked anti-Israel sentiments. In some reports there were indications that Iranian Jews had organized a branch of the terrorist network of the Haganah in Tehran and other provincial cities, and that the center of this network in Iran had transmitters and receivers and were in contact with the central organization in Palestine, sending messages in a special code and receiving orders in return. It was claimed that 60% of the cost of the Jewish terrorist organizations in Palestine were provided by foreign Jews living in Iran. Even the head of this terrorist organization (said to be someone by the name of Dr. Golpam) and those who helped Palestinian Jews had their names printed in the papers; i.e. Vahabzadeh, Shelimon, Mayer Abdellah, Katone, George Shaya, Safani, Lavi, Mashall, Salehe Moushi. These reports indicate that the Iraqi government protested to Iran about the voluntary arms shipments sent to Palestine by Iranian Jews. According to this report, another anti-Jewish organization under the leadership of Ayatollah Kashani was organized in every provincial city and developed a secret network in order to watch Iranian and foreign Jews. The aim was to use spies and information-gathering to supervise their communication and their methods of sending money, arms and volunteers from Iran to Palestine, in order to reveal them. Clearly these surveillance groups could terrorize, threaten or ruin those Jews involved in such activities. It was also said that Iranian Zionists bought arms from the southern tribes, especially the Qasghai and Boy-Ahmadiha, once used to fight against Iranian government agents, which were shipped from southern ports to Palestine. It was claimed that these arms sales via the southern tribes were done on the recommendations of the Americans, and that the tribes made lots of money and pleased the Americans who were the protectors of the Jewish terrorist organizations. In this provocative atmosphere, the Iranian government tried to keep calm, to maintain moderation, and did not let its policy become provoked by Ayatollah Kashani and his pressure groups and the religious sentiments of the people. The best indication of this moderate policy can be found in the speech of Hakimi, a former Prime Minister, in his interview with Agence France Presse in Tehran about a demonstration by some religious people and supporters of the Moslem Arabs of Palestine. Hakimi said that the problem of friendly demonstrations toward fellow Moslems, organized by some religious groups and mentioned in the papers, had no special meaning but only shows the natural sympathy which exists amongst Moslems throughout the world. Some of this positive sentiment which emerged from Iran during World War Two was based on the Nazi propaganda toward Hitler's Germany, and when Iran was occupied by foreign forces this sentiment remained like a fire smouldering under the ashes. Now these sentiments began to manifest themselves in a hatred toward Jews and sometimes in demands for the separation of Jews from the Iranian people. In the speeches of Ayatollah Kashani such anti-Semitic sentiments have without doubt a root in Shiite Islam and is very dependent on fascist sentiments which quickly reveal themselves. The topics that Ayatollah Kashani brought to public attention were the same problems that later Ayatollah Khomeini and his followers used in the struggle against the Shah. Kashani, in his speech for Arba'iin (the 40th day of the martyrdom of Hossein, the Shiite Imam) said "the economy of our country has been stolen by the Jews and Moslem trade has become dominated by a few Jews, and the millions in wealth of this country is concentrated in a few enemies of Islam. The authenticity of being Iranian is disappearing. Our money is being spent to eradicate

Moslems in order to increase their control over the economy of the country. If you want to understand this, just pay attention to our bazaar on a Saturday when you will see how the trade of our country comes to a standstill and all transactions stop. No one thinks about how we can rescue our economy from the hands of these few Jewish smugglers and how the houses of our brothers in Palestine have been occupied by Jews, or that their pride and chastity is under attack by Jews. Moslems of the world must sympathize with Palestinian Moslems and help them as much as they can. Is it right that the most wretched nation of the world stands against Moslems and commits this crime and we have to sit still?"

In this speech of Kashani two important points should be noted. First, his strong emphasis on the existence of the Jews in the bazaar and trade and second, the linguistic labelling he uses like the "most wretched country on earth" which clearly reveals the sentiments of Kashani and his followers.

On January 8, 1948, Kashani issued a communique against Israel in which he suggested war with the Jewish government and supplying arms to the Palestinian Moslems. This communique can be considered the first declaration of Jihad to which Ayatollah Khomeini was to appeal some thirty years later.

Kashani said in his communique that "from the day the U.N. gave an unjust mandate to divide Palestine and give part of its territory to a Jewish homeland for Jews immigration from Germany and the United States and other parts of the world, there has not been a day when some of your Moslem brothers have not been killed by Jews, and their houses and belongings were not being ruined and they were not being pushed out of their rightful homes. In the past few centuries there have been eighteen large and bloody wars in order to protect the soil of Palestine and thousands of Moslems have been killed but they didn't lose Palestine, which is the land of Moslems and Arabs. But now, the misfortune and wretchedness of Moslems has grown to such an extent that some smugglers and some homeless stragglers who have been thrown out of every country in the world have now, with the force of the great powers, decided to live on that land without any trouble to make part of Palestine their homeland. In order to gain control over Palestine they kill Moslem men and women every day. Now Jews who have power, wealth and arms have destroyed the lives of these poor Arab Moslems and wretched Palestinians who have no support in terms of power, wealth or arms. Villages, hamlets and the houses of Palestinians were ruined by Jews. All these Jews were homeless all over the world and their living and earnings were based on numerous crimes and tricks and they had no place as their own home. Now suddenly they want to govern Moslems and want to suck the blood of Moslems under their tyrannous hands. In this situation, the sacred religion of Islam obliges all Moslems to support the Moslem Palestinians and to sacrifice our lives and wealth for their cause."

Kashani opened a bank account and invited the public to make deposits to supply clothes and arms for the Arabs. His speeches and communiques in the Arab press were extremely popular. One interviewer in Al-Mesri noted Kashani's comment that "in my view, the shameful Israeli government does not pose any danger to Iran but we should not neglect the great danger which Israel poses to the Arabs."[14]

Kashani further organized meetings and demonstrations and brought the anti-Zionist and anti-imperialist issues into domestic Iranian politics. The Tudeh party supported Kashani on this question and recommended that their members participate in demonstrations, and in the party publications appreciated Kashani's activities against Israel, writing "From 1948 a new problem emerged which had no previous record; that is, the growth of sympathy with the Palestinian people and struggle against the Zionist government of Israel were suddenly considered of paramount importance. Some of the clergy, under the leadership of Ayatollah Kashani, led and organized this movement which expanded greatly over the spring and summer of 1948".[15]

On February 4th, 1949, a Tudeh member, carrying a press card of an Islamic paper in order to cover the graduation ceremonies at the University of Tehran, shot and injured the Shah. Later investigation showed that groups connected to Kashani had cooperated in terrorizing the Shah. Kashani was arrested and sent into exile. Tudeh protected his arrest and exile and party newspapers called this a retaliatory act by Abdolhossein Hazhir, the secretary of the royal court, who was "a member of the board of directors of the Bahaii sect" who wanted to show his utter dislike of Kashani's militant anti-zionism.[16]

When Kashani returned to Tehran, the Tudeh was jubilant and offered an alliance with all the forces gathered around him. The Tudeh paper **Besooye Ayandeh, (Toward the Future),** reported on June 9, 1950, about Kashani's triumphant return and said "amongst all the welcomers were many honest patriots who believed Kashani remained honest and loyal to the freedom fighters and supporters of democracy in Iran. Kashani would never cooperate with the enemies of the nation and would always maintain a militant stance against these enemies. We are very pleased that his unjust exile is finally over".[17]

It shouldn't be forgotten that Tudeh didn't only support Kashani for his militancy toward Zionism but also employed all their efforts to bring Kashani and his supporters toward other communist objectives. They printed some of Kashani's fatwa in the papers for the first time, and proposed a United Front of Anti-Imperialists. Eventually Kashani accepted the Tudeh's invitation to unity and said in an interview that "today is the time when men and women from every walk of life must be united in the struggle against foreigners. Today, the Iranian nation—that is all individual men and women, young and old, from all parties—have a shared goal in standing firm against imperialism."[18] In August 1952 Kashani's son formally announced their acceptance of the United Front of Anti-Imperialism.[19]

At the same time many Iranian nationalists influenced by Nazism and anti-semitism took advantage of the anti-Zionist mood to publish the Pan-Iranist Papers. The first page of a special issue for Noruz (March 1952) proclaimed "Workers of the world, enslaved by the chains of Jewish capital, rebel and free yourselves."[20] This bizarre coalition of Shiite clergy, Communists and right-wing extremists continued for many years and even after the 1978 revolution and the emergence of Khomeini the issue of Palestine and Israel continued to be a central thread of Iranian politics.

After the death of Ayatollah Hadj Agaha Hossein Bhomi, the leader of the Iranian Shiites, Ayatollah Borujerdi—who was a moderate and reasonable man—became the new Shiite leader. He tried to avoid conflict between the Shiite clergy and the political system, and prohibited Kashani's political activities and those of the terrorist organization, Fedaiin Islam, who had already conducted a few political assassinations. He banned the use of the pulpit for political speeches, especially about Palestine and the war with the Jews, and called the terrorist activities misguided tactics.[21]

Borujerdi openly stated that the only function of a Qum seminary student was to study, not to participate in political discussion and came to believe that the Fadaiin Islam threatened his own life.[22] He called Ayatollah Khomeini a "trouble-maker,"[23] and prevented him from teaching philosophy in Qum.[24] The improving relationship between Khomeini and Kashani from

1949, and their policy of rebellion and terror, was disrupted by Borujerdi.[25]

When Mossadegh became Prime Minister, Kashani postponed the idea of creating a United Islamic Organization and creating an Islamic Army to send volunteers to Palestine. As the conflict between the Shah and Mossadegh about the handling of nationalization of the oil industry developed through 1953, Kashani used the excuse of growing community influence to abandon the opposition to support the Shah. Kashani reacted by calling Khomeini a troublemaker who wanted to provoke a bloodbath.[28] The death of Kashani in December, 1961, and of Borujerdi in 1962, gave Khomeini a supreme opportunity to develop his ambition to step into the Shiite leadership without any serious obstacle to block his way.

In 1960, the Shah, in response to a press interview question about the relationship between Iran of the establishment of an Israeli government, was only de facto recognition. For economic and political reasons our government representative was recalled some time ago and has not returned." When the interview was published, Gamal Abdul Nasser developed a strong propaganda campaign against the Shah, using radio Sout Al Arab.[29] Turkey and the Soviet Union had also recognized the de factor existence of Israel, yet Nasser did not react against them and enjoyed close relations with the Soviets. Rather Nasser wanted a leadership role in the Moslem world and saw the Shah as a rival who had to be removed. Other nationalist Arab countries cooperated with Nasser in attacking the Shah. The Iranian residents of the Trucial states of the Persian Gulf were accused of plotting to take over Arab territory. Iraq, Syria and other Arab countries supported the independence movement of Iran's Arab population in an area where a major part of Iran's oil reserves were located; instead of calling that province Khuzestan they renamed it Arabestan. Nasser renamed the Persian Gulf the Arabic Gulf, and wanted to develop influence among the Trucial states, many of which were still under the auspices of the United Kingdom.[30]

When relations between Iran and Egypt were broken, it was widely regarded as a personal insult to the Shah. In his visit to the United States in June 1964, the Shah warned Lyndon Johnson and the Allied forces about Nasser's plan to invade Iraq and the western parts of the Gulf, and protested U.S. food aid to Egypt as furthering Nasser's ambitions. He asked for aid in order to improve Iran's defensive forces, particularly in Khuzestan.[31]

Nasser's opposition to Iran helped to unite the Arabs but also had repercussions on internal politics, since Nasser supported Khomeini's June, 1963 uprising and provided facilities and training camps for urban guerrillas in Egypt.

Khomeini increasingly argued that the entire White Revolution of the Shah was anti-Islamic and brought the issue of Iran-Israel relations to the fore. He mobilized demonstrations and religious gatherings through distribution of his tapes of speeches and his communiques and proposed that the clergy should take over control of the country.

When Kennedy became President of the U.S., bilateral relations worsened since the Democrats had never had very good relations with the Shah. On the other hand, Soviet propaganda and activities of those groups affiliated to Moscow mobilized opinion against the Shah. Nasser's activities continued and his foothold in Yemen created yet another problem for the Shah. Then too, Teymour Bakhtiar, the first director of SAVAK, was accused of plotting to overthrow the Shah and was dismissed and exiled to Iraq from where he provoked Khomeini's opposition.[32] The rest of the clergy also became involved with the Palestine issue. Ayatollah Mahmoud Taleghani had participated in the World Muslim Congress and anniversary of the Arab Republic in Egypt in 1959 and 1960, and traveled in other Arab countries. He was strongly influenced by Nasser and maintained a strongly anti-Zionist, pro-Palestinian stance.[33]

After the approval of the land reform articles in 1960 and the ratification of the law by the Majles under the government of Assodollah Aalam in September 1961, other new articles approving the social and political association of provincial cities, giving the vote to women, and requiring minorities to take the oath over religious texts were also approved. Khomeini continued propagandizing against the Shah, particularly arguing that Zionism jeopardized the economies of Islamic countries. He also brought attention to the Bahaii, calling them the fifth column of Israel.

In a communique in the fall of 1963, Khomeini declared, "I must warn all the Moslems of the world and the nation of Iran that the Koran and Islam are in danger, and the independence of the country and its economy have almost fallen into the hands of the Zionists in the form of the Bahaii party. It would not take too long for them to take over the entire country and rapidly impoverish the Moslem people. Iranian television is the spy center of Jews."[35]

In the winter of 1963, the Shah announced his plan for land reform which became the so-called "White Revolution." This land reform policy, which consisted of six articles, was approved in a nation referendum.

The approval of this reform significantly decreased the clergy's influence in national affairs, especially since a large tract of their endowed land was divided amongst farmers, but also because the workers became shareholders in the factories. The opposition to this policy included the Communists, the clergy, the big landowners and the bazaar merchants. The latter felt that with the development of the country that they would gradually lose control over economic matters, especially that import/export activities would be transferred to modern companies. Khomeini tried to be the leader of this emerging unity-in-opposition and on March 20th, 1963, the beginning of Noruz festivities, issued a fatwa which asked Moslems not to celebrate Noruz since Islam was in danger. This communique had little effect outside Qum.[36] As usual, Khomeini increased his accusations and criticisms against the Shah's regime and employed all his efforts to bring about conflicts between the police force and the people, especially with the theology students in Qum, so that it would become impossible to maintain law and order. In one speech, he accused the Israeli government that it had printed millions of forged Korans and distributed them in order to weaken religious belief. As Moharram and Ashura were approaching, he asked the clergy to explain to the people during their religious ceremonies about the danger and damage that Israel and the Bahaii meant for Islam in Iran.[37]

When Khomeini and his supporters realized they could not mobilize people through a critique of modernization, they changed to make Zionism a central point in the struggle against the Shah to the extent that they even brought the issues of Western culture and modernization under the banner of anti-Zionism. Fasafi, one of the most controversial clergymen of Tehran, in one passionate speech in 1962, said "our main problem in the election is not the participation of women about which the clergy has rebelled, but the real threat is that the Jews want to make another Palestine in Iran and to suffocate all the Moslems in this country and bring all the dirty elements of Bahaiism to power."[38]

Khomeini's attack on the Shah and the regime brought a great deal of turmoil to Qum, creating conflicts between demonstrators and the police. When these conflicts actually reached the ground of Feyzieh seminary, Khomeini became very pleased and said, "Finally, the regime has revealed its true colors, and this is what I wanted."[39]

At the same time, the Iranian Communists on one hand and the religious forces on the other were against the Shah's development strategy. The Shah labelled this conspiratorial opposition as the unity of "red and black," and in a trip to Qum publicity stated the relationship of Abdul Nasser, the President of Egypt, with the internal religious provocation in Iran. He said that "the objectives of these provocateurs is to establish a government like the Egyptian. They would say that they don't need an army, while the Egyptian government has spent over a thousand million dollars on arms. We helped 15 million peasants to become landowners but the Egyptian Nasser, the leader of this reactionary group, has at least 15 thousand political prisoners. He has no parliament, no elections, and now suddenly he has become the ideal man for the opposition. Now we are not free, but over there in Egypt the people are free."[40]

After the accusation against Khomeini as a traitor and cooperator with Nasser, Khomeini ordered all his clerical supporters that "from now on your chosen topics for homilies at religious gatherings should be addressed to the cooperation of the regime with Israel and the Israeli agents who are Bahaii."

In the religious mourning ceremonies for the Third Imam at Ashyra, the clerics did as Khomeini had asked and developed the slogans "The Israeli agents have been revealed" and "They have murdered the defenseless in Qum." Demonstrations spread to Mashad and in the beginning of June, a Khomeini supporter knifed a policeman. By the second of June, 1963, in Tehran, the religious mourning had been totally transformed into political demonstrations and the crowd shouted "Long live Khomeini;" "Death to the Shah." The leadership of the crowd was in the hands of a few vagabonds with knives. That afternoon Khomeini spoke from the minbar at Feyzieh Seminary in Qum and took a very hard line against the Shah, arguing in this speech that the Shah was selling the country to Israel and the Jews. The speech began thus, "Mr. Shah, don't obey the Israelis. Israel is no good for you. Israel is very dangerous for Islam and

Moslems, SAVAK tells us we should not talk about Israel. Tell me what is the relationship between you and Israel? What does it mean when Savak warns us not to talk about you or Israel? Does it mean that in the eyes of SAVAK the Shah is Israeli? Does it mean that in the eyes of SAVAK you are a Jew? Mr Shah, they wanted to introduce you as a Jew so that I could call you an atheist and throw you out of the country."[41]

On June 5th, large and bloody demonstrations by Khomeini supporters were held in Tehran and some other cities, which were later called the "second Ashura" and were the beginning of Khomeini's practical struggle to overthrow the Shah on behalf of the clergy. In these continuing demonstrations, various parts of the city were burnt and police stations, government offices, and private businesses owned by Shah supporters were all invaded. Telephone booths were removed, major cinemas ruined, and women employees without the veil or girl students on school buses were attacked, and a harsh struggle between the army, police and demonstrators developed. Government reported 74 people were killed (60 in Tehran and 14 in Qum), but Khomeinist sources claimed thousands had been killed. In the attacks on women and passersby, Khomeini supporters had developed a new tactic which they used in the revolutionary movement, arguing that the Shah's regime sent agent provacateurs out to burn down buildings and attack women in order to label the popular movement as backward and violent.[42]

Government officials after the 5th of June (15th of Khardad), tried to prove the connection of Khomeini with Nasser on the one hand and with big landowners on the other. General Pakravan, the director of SAVAK, said in press interviews that he had been confused about whether to take this group seriously or not, while Prime Minister Alaam, in documents which he showed to reporters, tried to prove that Nasser had a hand in the demonstrations. Tehran newspapers reported than an Egyptian agent, with a large sum of foreign money, had been arrested in Meharabad airport and had confessed that this was money from Nasser for some special individuals. Also, Al-Ahram in Cairo wrote on June 6th that Mahmoud Shaltout, the Sheikh of Al-Azhar, and a major supporter of Khomeini said that all the demonstrators wanted the Shah to fall and the end of the relationship with Israel.

After the bloody demonstrations of June 5th and 6th, Khomeini was arrested in Qum, imprisoned in Tehran but later released and returned to Qum, expressly against the agreement made with the security forces. He began his provocations again in an even harsher vein, developing an even stronger anti-Israel and anti-Jewish rhetoric. In a speech in March, 1964, he repeated again and again that "the economy of this country is in the hands of Israel and its agents, and all the factories, such as Arj, Pepsi-Cola, Iran Air, and also television are in Israeli hands. Today, even eggs are brought in from Israel. We have to cut the root of imperialism by cutting this relationship with Israel."[43]

Khomeini became interested in addressing the army and, for the first time in a speech, brought to the attention of the army the idea that Israel was penetrating the army; he argued that "every individual army member should throw Israeli agents and those who cooperate with them out of the army. Before there is no time left, we must put an end to these dangerous activities by the Israelis and their agents inside Iran."[44]

A year later, Khomeini became more active in the scattered opposition groups which were involved with terrorism throughout the country and developed a coalition amongst some of the Islamic groups under "The Islamic-allied Group." However, he also agreed to cooperate with the remaining underground supporters of Mossadegh, which brought him more support from the bazaar. He tried to silence those clergy in Qum and Tehran who disagreed with him, and built a new coalition with Nehzat-e Azadi, whose founders were Ayatollah Taleghani and Mehdi Bazargan. Later in the anniversary of June 6th events, the Khomeini supporters broke the mourning rituals and marched with banners that read "Israel should get its hands off Iran" and "We support Ayatollah Khomeini" through the streets of Tehran. When the Mojaheddin-Khalgh emerged as a group, they too supported Khomeini.

During this crisis, Alam resigned from the Prime Ministership and was replaced by Hasan-Ali Mansour. He took a bill to Parliament which allowed the American military advisors to be endorsed as technical specialists and thus come under diplomatic protection. When this will was ratified, Khomeini brought land reform and women's rights as crucial topics in his speeches. He beseeched "the leaders of Islam, come and help Islam. Oh, Ayatollahs of Najaf, help Islam The Ayatollahs of Qum, help Islam Islam is vanishing All the nations of Islam and their leaders, come and help us. We have been sold to the colonizers." This speech fifteen years later became the basis of foreign policy of the Islamic Republic, and the Students of the Imam's Line took 53 Americans hostage for 444 days with the slogan "U.S. is worse than England/England is worse than the U.S. The Soviet Union is worse than both of them Israel is the root of all our problems and the child of the United States!"[45]

Mansour had little choice, since the provocation and demonstrations organized by Khomeini became intolerable for the government, and decided to send Khomeini into exile. On November 4th, 1964, Khomeini was arrested in his home and was immediately sent to Turkey. SAVAK informed the public about his exile, saying "According to reliable information, Khomeini's method and provocative speeches were against the national interest and the security and freedom of the entire country, so it has been decided to send him to exile."

1. Shojaodin Shafa, *Jenayat va Mokafat,* Iranshar, Paris, 1986, 3rd vol, p. 1688
2. Richard Cottam, *Nationalism in Iran,* University of Pittsburgh Press, Pittsburgh, 1964, p. 84
3. Christain Pahlavan, "De l'amour La Haine: Iran et Israel", *Politique Internale,* 19, Spring, 1983, p. 94
4. *Mard-e-Emruz,* Tehran, December 20, 1947, p. 6
5. *Mard-e-Emruz,* Tehran, January 10, 1948, p. 4
6. Ibid
7. Ibid
8. Ibid
9. *Mard-e-Emruz,* January 24, 1948, p. 2
10. *Mard-e-Emruz,* February 7, 1948, p. 6
11. Cottam, op. cit., p. 11
12. *Donya-ye Islam,* January 10, 1948
13. *Atash,* January 9, 1948
14. Etela'at, Tehran, July 15, 1951
15. F.M. Javanshir, *Tadjrobeh-ye Bis-to Hasht Mordad,* Tudeh Party, Tehran, 1980, p. 47
16. Rassoul Mehraban, *Goushe-haye Tarikh-e Moasser Iran,* Atarod, W. Germany, 1981, p. 211
17. Javanshir, op. cit., p. 87
18. Ibid, p. 205
19. Ibid, p. 209
20. Cottam, op. cit., p. 85

21. *Yad,* Bonyad Tarikh Enghelabe Islami, Vol 2, no. 7, Tehran, 1987 pp. 22, 26, 27, 41
22. Ibid
23. Amir Taheri, Komeini, Balland, Paris, 1985, p. 111
24. *Yad,* Vol. 2, no 7, p. 37-8
25. Taheri, op. cit., p. 112
26. Ibid
27. Ibid, p. 117
28. Ibid, p. 124
29. Shojoadin Shafa, op. cit. p. 1688-91
30. Barry Rubin, *Paved with Good Intentions,* Penguin, Middlesex, 1981, p. 103
31. Ibid, p. 117
32. Taheri, op. cit., p. 124
33. Bahram Afrasiabi and Said Deghan, *Taleghani va Tarikh,* Niloofar, Tehran, 1980, p. 169
34. Seyyed Jaladin Madani, *Tarikhe Siayasi Moasser-e Iran,* Islamic Publications, Tehran, 1982, p. 382
35. Rouhollah Komeini, *Majmouye-i az Maktoubat, Sokhan-raniha,* Peyarnha va Fatvahaye Imam Komeini, Tehran, 1980, p. 11
36. Taheri, op. cit., p. 127
37. Ibid, p. 132
38. Ali Davani, *Nehzat-e Rouhaniyoun Iran,* Bonyad-e Forhangi Imam Reza, Tehran, Vol. 3, p. 149
39. Seyyad Hamid Rohani, *Nehzat Imam Khomeini,* Entesharat Raheh Imam, Tehran, 1360, Vol. 1, p. 251
40. Komeini, op. cit., p. 60
42. Rohani, op. cit., p. 488
43. Ibid, p. 656
44. Ibid, p. 697
45. Ibid, pp. 722-72

3

IRAN IN THE PROCESS OF REVOLUTION ISRAEL, SHAH, KHOMEINI

During 1978-9, when the monarchy collapsed and Khomeini came to power, the relations between Iran and Israel played an important role in the process. The scenario that Khomeini and his followers drew, was that the Shah is the friend of Israel and Zionism through economic, cultural, military and security relations with Israel—many of which are secret—and that the Jewish government would support the Shah as much as possible. They viewed the Shah as the one who sold the independence of Iran to Israel. Based on this interpretation,the opposition and revolutionary forces under the leadership of Khomeini stood against the Shah. They claimed that they wanted not only to gain freedom and liberty for Iran but also to regain Iranian independence. They tried to bring down the Shah, who was "the clockwork doll" of Zionism and Imperialism, and tried to unite all Islamic and anti-Zionist forces of the region and world, wanting eventually to change the balance of forces to the benefit of the Palestinians against Israel. But the same Shah who was supposed to be united with Israel said in July, 1975, in an interview with Heikal, the well-known Egyptian reporter, "In the war of 1967, Israel occupied Arab lands and refused to evacuate them. Many times I have told the Israeli officials who come to see me, that under no conditions do they have the right to occupy Arab land by force. Even if such a thing is undertaken by a nation with 20-30 million people, it is not right for a nation of 2 million to do. Unfortunately, they did not listen to me but rather began to criticize me very harshly in the Israeli press."

It is very hard to explain these conflicts which are totally contrary to the scenario of the Shah's opposition. In fact, the Shah had a military, economic and diplomatic relationship with Israel, but this relation was based on geo-political and regional security priorities.

On the other hand, this relationship was under constant pressure because Iran as an Islamic country never accorded Israel de jure recognition and never enjoyed full diplomatic relations. Furthermore, from 1973 on, the Shah's diplomatic relations were based on the improvement of relations with the Arab world and the support of Palestinian rights. Consequently, numerous conflicts emerged between Tehran and Israel. Israeli and Zionist media played a major role in promoting Khomeini and criticizing the Shah. And despite the revolution and rise of Khomeini to power, the two nations have had some sort of continuous relationship for the past forty years. Some writers and political analysts believed that Israel had played a very active role in bringing the Shah down to help Khomeini come to power.

The Israeli paper, Maariv, reported on February 16th, 1976, a discussion between Ezer Wiezman and Harold Brown, the US Defense Secretary. Wiezman asked, "Are you convinced that you can not blame Israel for the downfall of the Shah?," Harold Brown answered that the Shah was blamed for having diplomatic relation with Israel.[1]

Uri Lubrani, an Israeli diplomatic attachee in Tehran in 1974, said to a group of Americans visiting Iran, that the Shah's Regime was not in stable condition.[2] Although at that time, there was no sign of revolution in Iran, and the Shah was enjoying absolute power.

In the beginning of the upheaval the Israeli government was not supportive of the Shah's regime but in the spring of 1978 in their final analysis, they emphasized the fall of the Shah. A few months later, an Israeli agent went to Tehran to make sure that the forces loyal to the Shah would not terrorize Ayatollah Khomeini. The Israeli agent explained this mission by referring to the Ernest Junger Statement "that shooting Hitler would not stop the growth of Nazism but has to be ruined by the popular forces of the same people who brought Nazism to power."[3]

Finally, in November 1978, when the Shah was under attack by Khomeini, Syria, PLO and Leftists groups condemned the Shah because of his relations with Israel, especially military relations. The Voice of Israel, Kol Visrael 100, repeated the commentary of Western and Russian radio condemned the Shah for buying too much arms.[4]

On the other hand, when Khomeini came to power, Israel did change its regional policy and despite all Ayatollah's propaganda against Jews and the proclamation of jihad against the Jews, Israel still considered Iraq and Syria as her first enemies.[5]

Some other groups developed such extreme scenarios when they argued that the fall of the Shah was the result of a lack of cooperation between Mossad and SAVAK.[6] The major purpose was to bring about the collapse of the Iranian army which had the ability to stand against Israel.[7] This argument meant that in the final analysis it was the Shah's relationship with Israel which contributed in a major way to his downfall.[8]

The secret cooperation between Israel and the Khomeini Regime, particularly over arms sales and reorganizing the Ayatollah's army, will be discussed in the next chapter.

In order to understand the present relationship between the two countries, we have to examine the different periods in the 40-year friendship between the two nations. To clarify these periods, we will divide the Shah's reign in three phases:

1/From the establishment of Israel to Nasser's death, 1948-1970.
2/From Nasser's death to the Yom Kippur war, 1970-1973.
3/From the Yom Kippur war to the end of the Monarchy, 1973-1979.

1. As we've already mentioned, Iran only accorded Israel de facto recognition in 1950.

First, an office for Iranian Interests was established in the Swiss Embassy in Tel Aviv. One Swiss officer was in charge of the Iranian Interests section. Due to the gradual increase of Iranian Jews emigrating to Israel and their contact with that office, and the development of trade and other relationships, Persian-speaking personnel were needed. Therefore, the Swiss government requested that an Iranian officer be assigned to that office and the Swiss Embassy would introduce him as a Swiss diplomat to the Foreign Office of Switzerland.[9]

The Iranian government did this, but in 1951 when Mossadegh became Prime Minister, under pressure from Ayatollah Kashani and using the excuse of economic austerity, he recalled the Iranian officer to Tehran. He was never to return.[10] Ayatollah Kashani at that time said, in an interview by Al Masri, that Iran had definitely retracted its de facto recognition of Israel, but the relationship of the two countries was never cut off.

During the 1960's, Nasser severed diplomatic relations with

Iran because of Iran's relationship with Israel and Sheikh Mahmoud Shalout, the President of Al Azhar University, a most prominent religious figure in the Arab world sent a telegram to the Shah criticizing Iran's position. The Shah replied that the Ulema and the Islamic world should not be worried about Israel and her relationship with Iran, saying "I want to make sure our position supports Islamic ideals the rights of Muslims without considering race or tribe, and we have been consistent in all international organizations in support of the progress of the supreme Islamic objectives. In any incidents, no matter how small, even with the minority Cypriot Muslims, we have always been supportive. There is no need to remind you that when the problem of the Suez Canel came to the Security Council, the Iranian representative in the U.N. defended Egypt, and when the foreign forces invaded Egypt, the Iranian government condemned that invasion as anti-Islamic, and I personally insisted on the pulling-out of foreign forces from Egypt." The Shah emphasized that "Internal conflict, rumor-mongering and pessimism about some undocumented reports would harm the Islamic world; it is better to be precise and to the point."[11]

Nasser increased his hostility toward the Shah and in one of his speeches said: "the united Arab world would stretch from the Atlantic Ocean to the Arabian Gulf." He sent forces to Yemen as part of the extension of Egyptian nationalism and Pan-Arabism. Iran reviewed her political priorities in the region and because of Nasser's adventurism a new cooperation with Israel against Egypt brought the Israelis closer to Iran. This resulted in the reinforcement of the military up to 1966.[12] On numerous occasion, the Shah clearly mentioned that his closeness to Israel was the result of Nasser's behavior, and that it was based on defensive reactions against the Arabs, particularly their expansionist policies in the Gulf.

After the Six-Day War and the total military collapse of the Arabs in 1967, the Shah was the first world leader to roundly condemn the occupation of Arab lands, and whenever the Palestine issue was mentioned in the U.N., despite all the reports about Libya training Iranians in guerilla warfare, the Shah insisted on Palestinian rights and their demand for a homeland.[13]

In an interview with Eric Pace of the New York Times, the Shah said "Israel, like any other member of the U.N. has the right to exist in the same way as the Palestians have a right to a homeland." This view was based on Tito's first resolution of 22 November 1967, at the U.N. which asked for the return of occupied lands in return for recognition of Israel by the Arabs, which Iran strongly supported.[14]

Nasser, however, was not satisfied with the Shah's relation with Israel and accused him of supporting Israel during the Six-Day War.[15]

The decline of Nasser's influence in the Gulf region brought about better relations between the Shah and other Arab nations. The Shah wanted to resolve the issue of Bahrain which he previously brought to the U.N. and actually dropped his claim. In November 1966, he visited Saudi Arabia and resolved his differences about oil with Saudi Arabia. He also improved relations with Kuwait, and most importantly, Iran began to cooperate with the Arab countries of OPEC. However, another problematic incident occurred in the region. The Baath party in Iraq came to power in 1968 and relations between Iran and Iraq, which had been hostile for a long time, deteriorated even further. The threat of Iraq substituted for the threat of Egypt, and actually from the geographic point of view was a far worse threat. When the British left the Gulf, Iran took over the two strategic islands of Greater Musa and Lesser Musa.

In 1969, Nixon became President of the United States and supported Iran's increasingly important role in the Persian Gulf region. With the sudden death of Nasser in 1970, this period came to an end.

2. The phase from 1970-1973 witnessed an improvement in the bilateral relations as well as in relations with all Arab countries.

For example, in 1970, relations with Egypt restarted, through the sincere friendship of the Shah and Sadat which lasted until the end of their lives. A number of Arab leaders visited Iran to sign friendship treaties and the Shah visited Saudi Arabia, Kuwait, Jordan and the Trucial States. Also, OPEC with the Shah's cooperation played an effective role in increasing almost four-fold the price of exported oil. These massive oil revenues made Iran one of the most powerful nations in the Middle East.

The most important incident of this period is the Yom Kippur War of 1973 in which Egyptian and Syrian forces invaded Israel from the Suez Canal and Golan Heights, and in the first strikes, were able to achieve great successes. Here the Shah, for the first time, actively supported the Arabs, provided medical help to Jordan, gave logistical help to Saudi Arabia and allowed Syria's Russian planes to cross Iranian territory. Egypt also received oil from Iran. At the beginning, the Shah was not sure that the Egyptian forces could get from Barlev's defensive wall to the Sinai Desert, but when Sadat asked for oil, without hesitation the Shah provided help. The Shah felt the aid was correct in principle and believed that the military effort of Egypt was to regain the lands lost in 1967.[16] The Arabs employed all their efforts to use oil as a weapon against the U.S. and some other Western countries who supported Israel, and the oil embargo from October 1973 to March 1974, was highly effective. Iran was not prepared to participate in this embargo because the political platform of the Shah was based on the principle that oil was not a weapon but merchandise.[17] The Shah, in October 1973, despite his full support of the Arabs, facilitated Kissinger's peace mission to find an agreement between the Arabs and Israel, and was in a position to use his influence within the region to intervene and find a solution. However, the role he played was not particularly liked by the Russians who constantly tried to convince the Arabs of Israel's dangerous influence in the region.

3. The phase from 1973-1979 witnessed some political activities by the Shah who used his influence with the U.S. to solve the Palestinian problem and his speeches became much tougher about Israel. In one of those speeches, he mentioned that "I am not an enemy of Israel but can not accept the illegal occupation of land taken by force which even the U.N. has deplored." As a result, Iranian-Israeli relations were weakened.

Iran found a convenient political space to improve relations with Iraq when Saddam Hussein and the Shah met at the OPEC Summit Conference in Algeria in 1975 and the border conflicts were resolved. Israel became extremely unhappy. The Shah distanced himself from Israel and Mossad and slowly approached the Arabs, particularly Egypt, Iraq and Saudi Arabia.[18]

On 15 January 1975, the Shah, in an interview with the Austrian Die Presse, said the threat of a Third World War and the possibility of direct US interference in the Persian Gulf region provided an explosive environment and that it was Israel's refusal to recognize UN resolutions 242 and 338 which had created this situation.

Documents, published after the take-over of the US Embassy in Tehran in 1980, clarified the Shah's views on the region for the US State Department. For example, a document dated April 1974 said: "The Shah believed that the US must employ her efforts to prepare a reasonable solution for conflicts between Arabs and Israel. He is against the Jewish control of Jerusalem and supports the removal of Israeli forces from occupied territories, their return, and the return of Palestinians to their homeland." On February 5, 1975, in an interview with CBS network, he said: "It is said that by returning Sinai to Egypt, Israel would not have access to its oilfields and Iran should provide oil from now on. However, I am not a godfather of Israel. On principle, the oilfield of Abu Rudeis does not belong to Israel but to Egypt, and Israel has taken advantage of this oilfield. I am sure in the future, most of the oil companies would provide Israel with oil. The only problem is that Israel should pay the price."

A few days after this interview, on February 18th, the Shah met Kissinger in Zurich and told him to explain to the Israelis that if the oilfield of Abu Rudeis was returned, Iran would provide enough oil for Israel. In a press conference, he said: "Our policy about oil is that we sell to who ever pays us. When the oil tankers fill up, their destination is not important, because the sale of oil is purely an economic transaction." This was an important statement since Iranian oil could substitute for the oil of Sinai, although in a considerably more expensive manner.[19]

The Shah refused to cooperate with the 1973 oil embargo and was harshly criticized by other Arab OPEC members. Two years later, the Shah made the oil a powerful tool for regaining the occupied land with oil wells in Egypt. The Shah's open criticism of Israel in the region on one hand, and the rapid improvement of the Shah's relations with the Arab World on the other hand, caused tremendous concern for Israel. In July 1975, the Shah in an interview with the German magazine Stern said: "There is no military conflict directly between Israel and Iran because we do not have a common border, but I have to say that Israel is following a very unjust and inconsistent policy which is in conflict with UN resolutions and this policy must not continue." In this regard, from 1977, the Israeli Labor party lost the election and the Likud party took over. As a result, a conflict between the two Superpowers was inevitable.[20]

The Shah prior to the taking-over by the Likud party, said: "The extremism of the coalition government is high and I hope this does not pose serious problems." The policy of Israeli government, under the leadership Menachim Begin, was exactly opposite to the Shah's view. It can be said that Begin had a hostile policy toward the Shah, especially when the Shah insisted that the US should force Israel to evacuate the occupied land and to recognize the Palestinian rights. The Shah's persistence made the Israeli government very angry.

The foreign policy of the right-wing government of Israel became more opposed to the Shah.[21] During the discussions between Jimmy Carter, Begin and Sadat in Camp David, Begin tried to convince them that the Shah was finished and the time for helping him was over long ago.[22]

The change of heart toward the Shah from Tel Aviv happened slowly and was initiated by the right wing.[23] This change of position required a new policy in the region. Sadat said the Islamic revolution was the most striking blow to the Arab World and the acceptance of Camp David Accord.[24]

What was the new position?

Opening discussion with Israel directly by Egypt did change the regional policy of Israel which had held since the Suez crisis. The policy of the Israeli government was based on having close relations with non-Arab-countries of the region i.e. Ethiopia, Turkey, and Iran. The other reason was the Iranian army which was the only army in the Middle East which could over-come the Israeli military. They thought that after the revolution, the Iranian army would collapse and there would not be any threat to Israel. Also the Israelis knew that the Palestinians would go to Iran to help Khomeini to consolidate his power, and then perhaps in a short period of time Israel would have much less tension on her borders.[25]

In regard to the fall of the Shah, not only would Israel benefit from the security point of view, but she would also take advantage from the Khomeini revolution with the changing balance of power in the region and planting the roots of destabilization in the Arab World and particularly amongst those who were hostile to the Jews.

Khomeini was not the great leader of the Islamic World, since even among the Shiite leaders there were many who did not agree with him. Khomeini in reality was the head of the political clergy. During his exile in Turkey and Iraq, he was regarded as a political figure among the Palestinians and Egyptians. But after the death of Nasser, the establishment of diplomatic relationship between Egypt and Israel on the one hand, and the establishment of a friendship between Iraq and Iran, after 1975, Khomeini lost his major base of support and the only groups remaining were the Palestinians and the leftist groups of Iran. To a lesser degree he became dependent upon Syria and Libya. Khomeini was the leader of the minority Shiite which comprise only 10% of all the Muslems in the world and consequently his becoming a leader would create hostility and competition among Shiites and Sunnis, the majority perspective.

The continuous criticism of Khomeini to the leaders of Islamic countries and particularly toward Saudi Arabia prior to the revolution, created incredible tension and hostility between the Khomeini Regime and the Arab countries. Khomeini's communiques and books, particularly Velayate Faghih, which outlined a plan for Islamic government many years before the revolution, were distributed among the Hajj.

In South Lebanon, Khomeini also had friends and enemies, i.e. Imam Mussa Sadr and Ayatollah Khoii who was living in Najaf. Ayatollah Khoii was more senior and his followers were members of Amal, and were sympathetic to Khomeini but not his supporters.

Before the revolution, some thousands of Iranian students were trained by Palestinian organizations in urban guerrilla warfare. Most of these were communists and leftist sympathizers. Their temporary unity with Khomeini against the Shah was only to bring down the monarchy but afterwards created a lot of internal problems for Khomeini.

From 1975, the Iraqi government tried to limit Khomeini's activity. The secret police removed his pictures from the streets of Najaf and other Shiite cities, and then they forced Khomeini to leave Iraq. Khomeini could have gone to Kuwait but because he was hard-headed and stubborn he was not welcomed there, and ended up in Paris.

Khomeini's supporters and close contacts were members of Amal, some of the leaders of PLO, George Habash group, and Tudeh party. Many others, like Bani Sadr, Montazerei and Ghotzbadeh, were among his followers. This unharmonious grouping of people created internal rows inside the Khomeini Regime and kept Khomeini busy for some time. Focusing on Khomeini's danger for Israel while he divided Muslims brings us to a similar scenario that Israel had devised about Nasser. Mordechai Bentov, a cabinet minister of Israel, wrote in April

1972, that it was a dangerous story that the entire Jewish people could be endangered by Nasser and the Arabs. This was a fantasy which we made in order to start the Six-Day War to add more land to our country.[26] General Ezer Weizman, at the same time said in an interview: "I have to say that the danger of the elimination of Israel was not true."[27]

In the geopolitics of 1977-8, if Khomeini had not existed, Israel would have had to invent him.

1. Christian Pahlavan, "De l'Amour la Haine, l'Iran et Israel', *Politique Internationale,* 9, Printemps, 1983, p. 95
2. "Barry Rubin, *Paved with Good Intentions,* Penguin Books, Middlesex, 1981, p. 169
3. "Op. cit., p. 96
4. Ibid
5. Nazire Fanza, *Tehran Destin De l'orient,* Pierre Saurat, Paris, 1987, p. 53.
6. *"Shojaldin Shafa, Jenayat va Mokafata,* Iranshahr, Paris, 1986, Vol. 3, p. 1743
7. *Actuelles Valeurs,* Paris, 19 July 1982
8. Op. cit. p. 43
9. "S.J. Madani, *Tarikh Siyasi Moase Iran,* Daftar entesharat Islami, Qum, 1362, Vol. 2, pp. 168-169
10. Op. cit. p. 49 (FN)
11. Op. cit. Vol. 3, pp. 1690-1691
12. Shahram Chubin, *Iran's Foreign Policy 1960-1976; An Overview in Twenty Century,* ed. H. Amirsadeghi, Heinemann, London, pp. 198-199
13. Op. cit. Vol. 3, pp. 1693-1694
14. Safa Haeri, *Journal de Tehran,* 23, Sept. 1967
15. Op. cit. p. 94
16. Op. cit. Vol. 3, pp. 1693-1694
17. Op. cit
18. *Le Monde Diplomatique,* March 1979
19. Bernard Reich, *Quest For Peace,* Transaction Books, New Jersey, 1977, p. 308
20. Op. cit. p. 97
21. *Aharonot Yediot,* 12 January 1977
22. Op. cit. Vol. 3, pp. 1694-6
23. Houshang Nahavandi, *Le Grand Mensonge,* Nouvelles Editions Debresse, Paris, 1984, p. 107
24. Op. cit.

25. Op. cit. p. 108
26. *Al Hamismar*
27. *Ma'ariv.*, April 1972

4

ISRAEL REEMERGES IN IRAN'S POLITICS

In December 1978, the final efforts of the Shah were employed in finding a prime minister who would continue to maintain the monarchy, would be trusted by the White House, and supported by some opposition groups. Shahpour Bakhtiar accepted the post on December 28, 1978, based on the condition that the Shah should leave the country temporarily. The first signs of an official change in policy toward Israel emerged prior to the downfall of the Shah in January 1979 when Bakhtiar gave a report about his future cabinet.

Two central points of his policy were first, to expand and extend the political, cultural and economic relations with Islamic countries; and second, to establish friendly relations with Arab countries in regard to the problems of the Middle East and to support a homeland for the Palestinians, and to cancel the export of oil to Israel.[1]

During Bakhtiar's brief period of power, Yasser Arafat in a ceremony for the establishment of the 14th anniversary of Al Fatah said: "because of the revolution in Iran, we can say good-bye America and American interest." In reply to Brezinski, the head of NSC under Carter, who had said: "Goodbye PLO." Arafat rejoined that Ayatollah Khomeini promised that the Iranian revolution would support the Palestinians.[2]

Bakhtiar, without doubt, raised the issue of selling oil to Israel in order to satisfy the demand of Khomeini and repeated this problem again when he wanted to get the approval of Majles as prime minister. He also supported the idea that the military might of Iran in Persian Gulf should be put to the benefit of the Arab countries, particularly those who are hostile toward

Israel. Bakhtiar in his own book, "Ma fidlit", wrote that "In my last discussion with the Shah in the plane taking him to exile, we talked about the budget and equipment for the navy in the Gulf. I said that I disagreed with spending on expansion of military which has no benefit for Iran except for the contractors and the middlemen. I wanted to let the PLO open an office in Tehran but the Shah opposed that."

After the Shah left Iran in January 1979, Bakhtiar never had time to put his new policy into effect because on February 11th, the army refused to cooperate any longer.

When Ayatollah Khomeini came to power, Iran's relationship with Israel was cancelled. The Fedaiin, Mojaheddin and Tudeh were all anti-Israel, had been trained in Palestinian camps in Lebanon, and many clergy shared these views. Even then a group of Iranian Jews called the Jewish Youth Organization and Organization of Jewish Intellectuals participated in anti-Shah demonstrations from January 1979 to support Khomeini and stated their hatred of Zionism and Israel.[3] The struggle with Israel became one of the major slogans of the Islamic Revolution.

After the Shah, PLO gave more information about their relationship with the political opposition and practically demanded a greater share of power in the revolution, i.e. Ahamd Jebrail, the military leader of the Popular Front for the Liberation of Palestine, in an interview with AP reporter in Damascus said: "From 1970, the PLO made close contact with Iranian revolutionaries and more than ten leaders have been trained here." Qaddafi also mentioned that he had supported the Iranian revolutionary forces. Jebrail added that the main objectives had been gained in the downfall of the Shah and the ending of relations with Israel.

Farokh Kaddoumi, speaker of the PLO, said: "we have a direct relation with Ayatollah Khomeini" but was not ready to give further information. AP reported that a group went to Paris to consult with Khomeini, but did not reveal the content of the meeting.[6]

On the 11th of February 1979, after the collapse of the armed forces and police, the revolutionary forces took over the Israeli Interest Office on Kakh Street in Tehran. Armed men invaded the building and looted whatever was inside then draped the red flag on the top of the building. During the Shah period, they never allowed to put the sign of the Israeli Embassy there.

On 18th of February, the headlines of Tehran newspapers said: "Arafat has returned home."

Arafat was the first foreign dignitary to visit Iran after the revolution, coming without a prior invitation in his own private jet and said he felt his visit to Tehran was equivalent to visiting Jerusalem. When asked why he didn't inform Tehran that he was coming, Arafat answered: "When someone goes to his own house, it's not news." From Mehrabad Airport, he came under the protection of the Mojaheddin and some Palestinians and went directly to see Khomeini. The visit was reported as follows, "Arafat, the leader of the PLO, arrived in Tehran with his private jet, and Hojjat-ol-lslam Haj Aghah Ahmad Khomeini, the son of Ayatollah Khomeini was the first person to welcome him. His visit with Imam Khomeini was a historic moment. They gazed at each other, then hugged. Khalkhali, Ayatollahs Rabbani-Shirazi and Sanei, and Dr. Ebrahim Yazdi were present too. Negotiations between Imam and Arafat took two hours and many important issues were left for later on."[5]

Arafat's trip was supposed to take three days but was extended to six. The group accompanying him was 59 persons and one group was Palestinian women commandos, with medical, public relations, and press groups also. The Israeli embassy, which had been taken over on the first day of the revolution, was opened by Arafat as a Palestinian embassy with great ceremony in the presence of Barzargan, the Prime Minister, and Sanjabi, the foreign minister, and Yazdi the vice-prime minister. The name of the street was changed from "Kakh" to "Palestine." Arafat also met Ayatollah Taleghani, his closest friend in Tehran, and traveled to Mashad and to Ahwaz, a heavily populated city of Khuzestan where he opened a PLO information office. Arafat's relationship with Taleghani was very important for Taleghani's commitment to support the Palestinians because it is a much longer one than that of Khomeini or Bazargan. Later the differences between PLO and Amal in Lebanon appeared in internal Iranian politics with Mostafa Chamran, the head of Information and Security of Khomeini, Abbas Zamani (Abu Sharif) the first commander of the Pasdaran and supporter of Habash in competition with the PLO. Taleghani said during Arafat's visit that, "At this moment the right hand of Israel has been cut but it is your responsibility, Mr. Arafat, to cut the other hand in Jerusalem. Neither you nor we ever imagined that we would have a meeting in Tehran. I do not know if I am dreaming or I am awake."[6] Taleghani introduced his children to Arafat and said they were at his disposal until the final victory.

All the friendly and complimentary complements of Khomeini to Arafat was not a real answer to the PLO demands because they wanted to have political support and practical base in terms of arms, money, and human resources. Khomeini said Arafat had achieved two victories one in Lebanon and the other in Iran, but Arafat replied that "the people of Palestine and myself have donated our blood for Palestine and will continue. We want you to give us more help and more resources."[7]

The PLO had discovered that they could not expect as much from Khomeini as they had invested in the downfall of the Shah. Khomeini made it clear that the internal problems of Iran and the rebuilding of the damage created by the Shah, put the Islamic Republic in a weak position which made it unable to help the Palestinians very much, and left these issues to be resolved in the future.[8]

Thus, the Islamic Republic's support for PLO was verbal, not material. The only real agreement made between Bazergan and Arafat was that, since most of the expatriates had left Iran, Palestinians would be welcomed to work in the oil industry.[9] Amir Entezam, the vice prime minister, in an interview on April 12, 1979, said: "Iran had made no decision to arm the Palestinians and is not concerned to use the Palestinian proletariat in the military or military-industrial complex. We will fully support them in international organizations." In September, Ebrahim Yazdi, in answer to a question about whether Iran would give arms and forces to the PLO, said that Iran was ready to do so but the Palestinians had not requested this yet.[10]

During this period, numerous incidents inside Iran very much concerned the Israelis, i.e. Khomeini in January 1979, in Paris sent a huge bouquet of flowers to the great Jewish chachom in Tehran and in a letter accused the Shah of mistreating religious minorities in Iran. He mentioned that although he wanted no political relations with Israel, he guaranteed that Iranian Jews could live and worship in Iran in a much better manner than under the Shah.[11] But in less than three months after the establishment of the Islamic Republic intimidation and harassment of Jews started everywhere. By May 1979, through direct orders of Khomeini, Habib Elghanian, one of the wealthiest and most popular Jews in Iran, was accused of being a Zionist and aiding the Israeli army in bombing Palestinian camps and assisting in the massacre of militant Palestinians. In a mock trial Elghanian said in his defense "I am proud to be an Iranian Jew, I have never spied to the benefit of Israel and have never aided them. I have never agreed with the massacre of Palestinians."[12] Nevertheless, he was executed.

Later throughout the country there were stories of numerous executions of Jews, and their houses were bombed and their wealth confiscated. It was clear to most Jews that if any Jewish family would be arrested, the accusation of being Zionist was inevitable. Yet Henry Precht, in charge of the Iran Desk in the State Department, accused Stefan Rosenfeld, the Washington Post reporter who had called Khomeini an anti-Semite, of inaccurate reporting.[13]

The turmoil of revolution and the different statements of different groups around Khomeini and the lack of clear foreign policy created tremendous tension within Arab countries with the two exceptions of Syria and South Yamen.

Khomeini called the 17th of August, the day of Quds (Jerusalem Day) and in a communique, requested all the Moslems of the World to participate in a demonstration for the commemoration of Palestian rights, but there was no very positive response to his demand.

The Arab countries in the region became irritated by the statements of Khomeini and some of the clergy close to him about the Islamic Revolution. They came to the conclusion that the new Iranian regime would create tremendous instability in the region, particularly in Bahrain, Kuwait and Iraq. So, after a short period of tranquility, Iran's relations with the Arab countries, particularly the sheikhdoms, became very tense until the war between Iraq and Iran began.[14] This conflict was the result of the weakness of the Bazargan government and the lack of concrete foreign policy. Amir Entezam, the Speaker of the government, in May 1979, answered an Iranian reporter about the relations between Iran and Israel by saying: " We don't have any relation with Israel, but if we did, it would be very superficial. I think the relationship has been cancelled; let me check and I will tell you next time."[15] And this was after the formal severing of ties with Israel on February 18, 1979!

On a formal visit by Sheikh Sabah Al-Ahmad Al-Sabah, the Foreign Affairs Minister of Kuwait, in July 1979, in a meeting with Ebrahim Yazdi, the Foreign Affairs Minister of the Islamic Republic, stated Kuwait's desire for the formal re-establishment of friendship with Iran. But, this agreement didn't get very far and in October of the same year, Iran asked Syria and the PLO to help her improve the relationship between Islamic Republic and the Gulf Arab states. Consequently, a group of PLO under Abu Jihad and a group of Syrians under the leadership of Khadam, the Foreign Minister of Syria, traveled between Iran and the Arab countries of the region to try and improve relations. However, this was unsuccessful and the PLO was not able to help the Islamic Republic.[16]

On April 30th 1979, under Khomeini's direct authority, diplomatic relations with Egypt were severed because of the Camp David Accords. Later when Arafat couldn't help to improve the foreign relations of the Islamic Republic, he lost status in Khomeini's eyes. On one occasion, Hani-ul Hassan, the PLO man in Tehran, asked Ayatollah Taleghani to send someone to the Palestinian embassy to receive a special message from Arafat. Taleghani sent one of his sons, who had a Palestinian wife. Hassan explained that the PLO had been told to close its office in Ahwaz, the capital of Khuzestan, the opening of which had been approved by the Revolutionary Council and Ahmad Khomeini. Arafat had replied that if this was the situation, then the PLO would prefer to withdraw totally from Iran. Taleghani's son was told to explain the situation to his father and that the PLO was waiting for his advice. Returning home, Taleghani's son was arrested by revolutionary guards. In protest, Ayatollah Taleghani closed his own office in Tehran and went into seclusion. Tehran and some other cities experienced some turmoil and the Mojaheddin Khalgh held some stormy protests. Finally, Khomeini personally requested through Ahmad Khomeini that Taleghani return to Tehran.[17]

Government officials mentioned on numerous occasions that the PLO and PFLP in particular, were provoking the Arab minority in Khuzestan, that in the conflicts between Iran and Iraq they were supporting the Iraqi forces, and also the Fedayi inside Iran. Admiral Madani, the governor of Khuzestan and the commander in chief of the navy, accused Habash for the turmoil in Khuzestan. Ayatollah Shariat-Madar, the grand Ayatollah, on numerous occasions said that it was not right for security reasons that the Palestinians have an office in Khuzestan.[18]

In the Iranian press, the different groups supporting Palestinians and Amal criticized government officials about this issue, i.e. a pro-Palestinian magazine wrote on August 20, 1979, that Arafat and Habash had argued bitterly about the latter's involvement in Khuzestan. Consequently, the PFLP finally sent a group with forged passports to provoke separatist sentiments in Khuzestan.[19]

In Iran, the different political and religious groups inside and outside government, i.e. the communists, separatists, moderates and extremists were all in a bitter struggle about these matters. Every day, scores of people were executed and hundreds were killed in the course of political struggle.

Khomeini accused the United States of creating unrest and provoking anti-imperialist feelings, and there was a race between him and the left about the production of anti-American slogans. The government cancelled many military and trade agreements with the US, amongst the most important being a five-year agreement for military hardware amounting to 9 billion dollars which was signed during the Shah's reign but was cancelled in August, 1979. Then, Iran refused to receive Walter Cutler as the new ambassador. Despite this rejection, Carter on October 5, 1979, said the shipment of spare parts of military planes had started again.[20]

The most important incident in this period was the admittance of the Shah to Cornell Hospital in New York for cancer treatment on October 22, 1979. Khomeini's regime was becoming isolated and Iranians were becoming disillusioned by the way he was handling the situation, and suddenly, Khomeini accused the US of supporting the Shah and trying to overthrow the Islamic Republic.[21] Then, on November 4th, a group of students, calling themselves Students of the Imam's Line, invaded the US Embassy and took over a hundred hostages, including diplomats, embassy workers and others. Fifty-two were kept for 444 days, until January 20, 1981, when Ronald Reagan became President.

Jimmy Carter stopped the shipment of spare parts to Iran on November 8, 1979. After five months, on April 1980, diplomatic relations were severed and the economic sanctions against Iran became inevitable. The hostage taking not only had a direct effect on Iran's relations with other countries but had a serious impact on their relations with the PLO.

Arafat with Sa'ad Sayel and a group of PLO officials visited

Iran on the first anniversary of the revolution and participated in a military march, although Taleghani had already died. The welcome and support for the PLO by the Fedayi guerillas and the Mojaheddin, because of their conflicts with Islamic Republic, was more sincere than that of Khomeini. Rajavi, the leader of the Mojaheddin, in welcoming Arafat, gave him a Uzi machine-gun that one member had taken from Iranian security forces and said: "It was the Palestinian revolution which first acquainted us with weapons. For none of us is the struggle against Zionism finished. Please accept this machine-gun as a trophy in the hope that one day we will all meet in Qods."[11]

There were different reports about the agreement between Khomeini and PLO for payment of a two dollar share of every barrel of oil barrel to the PLO.[22] From April, 1980, the sign of conflict between Khomeinind PLO emerged, i.e. A Palestinian mission in a conference in Iran accused Khomeini's regime about returning the three islands in the mouth of the Persian Gulf to the Arabs. Then Islamic Republic's radio and television was astonished by this statement by the PLO missions in Iraq.

In November, 1980, the real honeymoon between Khomeini and Arafat was over. Later on, PLO sent a group to Tehran to mediate about the hostages, but Khomeini even refused to meet them while this mission was under the leadership of Arafat.

The students of the Imam line said; "there is no negotiation and mediation for hostages possible." When Hani-ul Hassan, the Palestinian ambassador thanked Khomeini for accepting the request of PLO to release the black woman hostage, one of the speakers of Khomeini's office confirmed that Khomeini did not meet with PLO's representative and he said the statement of the PLO representative in Tehran was a fabrication because PLO wanted to take advantage of improving his relationship in Washington.[23] As a result of this, Yassar Arafat's great hope for mediation of the hostages crisis on one hand and the improvement of his relationship with Washington on the other, had gone by the wind.[24]

During 1979 and 1980, when the war broke out between Iran and Iraq. Iranian army and Iranian security forces were under attack by Khomeini. Most of the armed forces leaders and many others were discharged and some fled the country. The Islamic Republic organized another military organization along with arms, a police security force, which were called Revolutionary Pasdar, and Revolutionary Committee and Savama.

The Summer of 1980 was a season of struggle, a season of disastrous conflicts, a period of exile, a period of real turmoil. To the extent that almost the entire regime had lost its common sense. The Islamic Republic was upset that the Shah was in Egypt and his active opposition, i.e. General Oveisi, and Bakhtiar in France, all launched a propaganda campaign against Khomeini. They organized clandestine radio in Iraq to mobilize for the overthrow of Khomeini.

These propaganda efforts had incredible impact inside Iran and made Khomeini's regime very confused. They were purging the army and Khomeini continuously gave interviews and warned the people that the CIA, Mossad, Intelligence Service and the former Savak agents and opposition and exile leaders all wanted to overthrow the Islamic Republic.[25]

The Herald Tribune in June 10 and August 16, 1980 wrote that Khomeini has organized a new information office which is active inside and outside of Iran and is under the supervision of General Fardoust.

Finally, Islamic Republic on May, 1980, claimed that one military coup by Oveissi and other Generals of the previous regime had been discovered. On June 12, another plot was discovered and again on June 22, another plot by Bakhtiar with the cooperation of Iraq was discovered. Each time, many people, particularly military personnel connected with those plots, being executed or imprisoned.

The most important plot discovered was on June 9, 1980. According to Khomeini's claim, the airforce was to take control of Nuzheh airbase. This base was close to Hamadan. The airforce was to strike Khomeini's residence, Fazieh seminary school in Qum, and Tehran airport. This plot was discovered when a group of pilots were going to Hamadan. Six hundred of those airforce officers were arrested. In June and July, 81 of them were executed.[26]

Twenty months after Khomeini took power, on September 22, 1980, the Iranian army was in poor shape, particularly the airforce, because the best pilots and technicians had been executed while others were in hiding after a military coup. The country was in a mess.

Despite Khomeini's total elimination of relations with Israel and even his claim to want to occupy Quds, yet even after the revolution there were some trade relations and contacts between the two countries. The source of these rumors was usually the opposition in Europe and the US. One opposition paper in Paris reported an international company, located in Tel Aviv, called Overseas International Supplies, sold kerosene to Iran which had a shortage. The Iranian government endorsed the shipment and President Carter said that he had agreed to the sale, but the exact name of the company which sold the kerosene never appeared. It was also claimed that many top Iranian officers who had contacts with Mossad or some training in security from Israel prior to the revolution, got important positions in the army and Savama. Consequently, there was a kind of security operation between the two countries. One of these high-ranking officers was Major General Hossein Fardust who was the Security Advisor to Khomeini. Another was General Hossein Shaker who became the Chief of Staff of the Slamic Republic and Major Colonel Farazian who was the previous Director of Savak and his assistant Major General Kaveh. It was also reported that Israel was selling food, especially chicken and eggs, to Iran.[27]

The Washington Post wrote that the exile opposition group complained that Mossad pretends that the opposition is trying to overthrow the Islamic Republic but in reality the regime is creating problems for the opposition.[28]

Later in the opposition paper, two names dominated the headlines, those of Manouchehr Ghobanifar and Cyrus Hashemi. An Iranian military man who had participated in a failed Nuzheh coup on 9th July, 1980 and fled the country, wrote that "the go between officer from the center of the coup in Paris with the other coup leaders in Tehran was called Manouchehr Ghobanifar. He was introduced as Hajj Ghabani and in Turkey he had a different name and a different one in Paris. He was responsible for providing arms for officers who participated in the coup in Tehran. He was in contact with most of the top officials of the government and the clergy. He tried to solve the problem of friends and individuals with the revolutionary committees. He always discussed his close contact with top officials of Khomeini's regime and at the same time had close contact with Paris."[29] It is likely that Ghobanifar or an associate prior to the coup had given all the information secretly to Bani-Sadr the president at that time. Bani-Sadr after discovering the 9th July coup plan, said: "One of the main sources who had a hand in the plot had met with him in the Tutti Garden and provided the names of participants."[30]

At the same time, the opposition in the US said Cyrus Hashemi, who had an office in 9, W. 57th Street in New York, was in charge of the security organization of Khomeini, Savama. According to this source, Hashemi and his brother Reza were active in student organizations which supported Khomeini in the US. Also, the source indicated, Hashemi was in charge of providing arms for Tehran and other terrorist groups in the US and Europe against the opposition.

In that time, this news did not attract much attention but a few years later in 1986, Ghobanifar became very well-known as an effective mediator in the secret arms transactions of arms with the US, Israel and Iran- so called Iran-gate- as did Cyrus Hashmi, the other arms dealer between Israel and the Islamic Republic. Hashemi, on July 21, 1986, just prior to the Irangate crisis, died in curious circumstances in London.

1. Ismail Charles Semkus, *The Fall of the Shah 1978-9,* Author, US 1979, Vol. 2, p. 567
2. Iranian Press, Jan. 9, 1979 (according to AP from Beirut)
3. Semkus, op. cit. p. 633
4. AP. Damascus, Jan. 20, 1979
5. *Ettela'at,* Tehran, Bahman 29, 1357
6. Bahram Afrasiyabi and Said Dehghan, *Taleghani and Tarikh,* Nilufar, Tehran, 1360, pp. 410-412
7. David Menasheri, "Report on Iran", *Middle East Contemporary Survey,* Vol. 3, 1978-79, Helms and Meier, New York, p. 541
8. *New York Times,* 27 February, 1979
9. Semkus, op. cit. p. 782
10. *Al Nahar,* October 1979
11. Semkus, op. cit., p. 615
12. Keyhan Havaii, Tehran, May 16, 1979
13. Christian Pahlavan, "De L'Amour la Haine, l'Iran et Israel", *Politique Internationale,* No. 9, Printemps 1983, p. 101
14. Menashri, op. cit., p. 538
15. *Kayhan Havaii,* Tehran, May 16, 1979
16. Manashri, op. cit., p. 540
17. Afrasiyabi and Deghan, op. cit., pp. 438-448
18. *Al Hawadeth,* Juin 22, 1979
19. *Omid,* Tehran, Aguust 21, 1979, p. 50
20. Barry Rubin, *Paved with Good Intensions,* Penguin, Middlesex, 1981, p. 370

21. Abolhasan Bani-Sadr, "De L'Exil L'Espoir", interview in *Politique Internationale,* 14, Winter, 1981-2, p. 258
22. *Mojahed Weekly,* Tehran, February 8, 1980
23. *Sunday Times,* 18 March, 1980
24. Menshari, op. cit., p. 482
25. Pierre Salinger, *America Held Hostage,* Doubleday, New York, 1981, pp. 51-52
26. *Jomhuri Eslami,* Tehran, May 15, 1980
27. Menashri, op. cit., p. 471
28. Iran Azad, Tehran, 11 October, 1980
29. *Washington Post,* 17 May, 1980
30. Iran Azad, 20 December 1980

5

IRAN-ISRAEL RELATIONS AND THE BEGINNING OF THE GULF WAR

Iran-Iraq war broke out at 1:30 pm, on September 22, 1980 after a harsh exchange of political slogans. The Iraqi, planes in the first hour of the war, bombed airports and important cities. The Iraqi infantry also entered Iran across 500 kilometers of shared border.

The start of this war provided special opportunities for extensive military cooperation between Israel and revolutionary government of Iran. As a result of this war, Israel achieved her goal which was the weakening of military force in Iraq.[1]

The importance of the Iran-Iraq war was felt to be of such tremendous interest for Israel that some sources even claimed that Israel facilitated the start of the war. Abol-Hasan Bani-Sadr claimed that Israel had a provocative role in the beginning of the war. When he fled to Paris in June 1981, he wrote in his paper, the so-called "Islamic Revolution in Exile" in October 1982 about the starting of the war, that according to the information he received, Iraq had played a role in the Accordion plot with the cooperation of Israel. The aim of the plot was firstly to encourage Iraq to attack Iran and, on the other hand, with the cooperation of Lebanese Phalange, to chase out the Palestinians from Lebanon. Bani-Sadr maintained that he was told by Mr. Yasser Arafat about this plot before Iran-Iraq war broke out. In his article, he claimed that prior to the war he had asked Yasser Arafat to go to Baghdad and persuade Saddam Hussein not to invade Iran. Arafat was aware that Israel with cooperation of the Lebanese Phalange wanted to carry out the Accordion plot. He claimed that he did his best not to let war happen, but instead not only was war started by Iraq, but also Israel invaded Lebanon in 1982 in order to disarm the Palestinians and to provide the background for the Kataeb (Copts?) to rule in Lebanon, which was also part of the Accordion plot."

But Bani-Sadr was not the only one who claimed that Israel had from 1980 played a provocative role between Iran and Iraq or wanted to have a military and political relationship with Iran. The Israeli newspaper Ha'aretz on December 18, 1980, wrote "from July 1980, the Jewish lobby in the United States played an active role in persuading the U.S. to send military parts to Iran in change for the freedom of hostages." Even some internal sources of the Israeli government who do not want their identity to be known, believed that military cooperation between Israel and Iran after the fall of the Shah never really stopped. Another trusted source in Israel said "Israel secretly from the time of the fall of the Shah in 1979 has already provided military parts to Iran."[2]

It was certain that most of the Western industrial countries put the Islamic Republic of Iran on an economic embargo from a few months before the war, because of the hostage-taking. Thus, when the war started, Iran had no other choice but to begin to buy arms and military equipment to organize the revolutionary Pasdar and the new security military and revolutionary forces. Consequently some of the highest members of the government made a lot of money in these lucrative arms transactions. Ali-Reza Nobari, the former head of the Central Bank of Iran, in regard to the economic crisis of Iran after the revolution, complained about the massive expenditure on arms. On 16 January 1980, he wrote to Behzhad Nabavi, the vice-Prime Minister and the man in charge of negotiations for the release of the American hostages, giving a warning hint that the amount of arms and military equipment being ordered from foreign countries would reach $3 billion.[3]

"The Iranian military forces during the Iraqi invasion in September 1980 were very disorganized and chaotic, and were not able to defend the border or even to bring about law and order inside the country. Besides a few nationalistic rebellions in different parts of the country, such as Turkomansahra, Azarbaijan, Kurdestan, Khouzestan, and Baluchestan, had made the country ready for internal conflict and civil war. The clash between Khomeini and Bani-Sadr about selecting a Prime Minister emerged when Khomeini wanted Rajaii while Bani-Sadr refused to accept him.[4] In regard to the border clashes with Iraq, Khomeini was afraid of mobilizing the army and did not believe that war was imminent or that any country could invade Iran. He assumed that any rumors of invasion were designed to remove the revolutionary leaders in the army.[5]

Bani-sadr wrote about the armed forces, "the army was under various pressures. When I asked the infantry commander to take responsibility, he answered that there were no infantry forces to command because all the tanks artillery guns, and carriers have been abandoned for over a year without repairs. In all of Khuzestan, there were only 28 tanks. What remained of the ground forces were scattered all over the country and because of the war in Khuzestan and the hostile relations of the government to the tribal leaders the ground forces were not able to get involved in a serious war. In addition, all three forces, ground, air and navy, because of the shortage of military parts are not able to go on any missions."[6]

Most of the officers of the air-force, which had been one of the most effective arms of the forces of the country under the Shah, and the navy were purged even though these two forces did not participate in killing demonstrators under the Shah. During the Shah's time, the Air-Force could use only 40% of their planes and many more were damaged during the mass movement. The Tudeh and other communist groups penetrated and ruined a great deal. Only 60% of the F-5, 40% of F-4 and 10% of F-14 could be used. With the start of the war with Iraq, because of the lack of parts, some planes had to be used for parts thus further decreasing Iranian strike-power.

On the one hand, the clergy was purging the army and on the other, the internal conflict between Khlkhali, the hanging judge, and others inside the regime purged 7500 officers and military personnel in the armed forces. The representatives of military groups started to demonstrate on the streets of Tehran and asked for the purge of their commanders, i.e. 500 technicians and parachutists of ground forces in February 1980 demonstrated in front of the Heart Hospital where Khomeini was, demanding the purge of all officers in the army and the organization of Islamic Councils in all three forces. The air-force officers went to the mosque of Tehran University and sat-in, demanding the return of all high-ranking officers and an end of the purges.[7] The English magazine, *Military Balance*, estimated that in 1979-1980, 60% of military personnel had quit and in some infantry units this had reached 80%. The navy at the start of the revolution had less purging but many officers and specialists trained in foreign countries were later purged, imprisoned or fled the country.

In less than two years, three navy commanders, Alavi, Madani, Tabatabaii, were purged based on allegations of spying for the USA and imperialism, Admiral Alavi was imprisoned and a televised military court accused him and then Madani fled the country. The Islamic Regime was very suspicious of the westernized dependent navy, and during the Iraqi invasion the navy commander happened to be a Marxist and member of Tudeh called Bahram Afzali. He was commander of an active unit of the navy and together with his colleagues he was arrested based on CIA information and was executed after a very short military court. Because of the historical, cultural and ideological tendencies in the Iranian armed forces, they were not able to cooperate with the clergy. The Iraqi attack came at the worst psychological moment and the forces were quite lame.[8] In order to understand how much the armed forces were disorganized and scattered, Khomeini out of desperation in February 1980 made Bani-Sadr, a man with no military background whatsoever, the Commander-in-Chief of the armed forces.

The new revolutionary government was very hostile to the armed forces because they saw them as the remains of the previous regime. The discovery of numerous plots in the Armed Forces made the army weaker day by day. Three plots were discovered exactly when the war with Iraq started, ie.

1/a terror network was discovered but the arrest of the members was kept secret.

2/a network related to Shapour Bakhtiyar, according to a claim by the Islamic Republic, was uncovered and a group of military and civilians arrested.

3/another groups was called Neghab (Cover) and most of this group were Air Force officers and special task force personnel.

Over one hundred of them were arrested. The government announced that these groups were engaged in a coup d'etat plot.

The regime claimed on 23 May 1980 to discover preparations for a coup by Oveysi and other senior officers. Another plot was reported on 12 June. On 22 June, the regime gave details of yet another plot, this time by Bakhtyar acting in coordination with Iraq...

The most serious coup attempt was scheduled for 9 July. Tehran reported on 10 July that officers of the Air Force were to have taken over the base at Hamadan (in Western Iran) and to send out aircraft to bomb key targets, including Khomeini's home, the Qom Theological Seminary and Tehran Airport. In these "plots", about 600 men were arrested.[9]

The mass arrest in the armed forces on one hand, and the failure of Desert One in April 25, 1980 (the rescue mission in Tabas Desert), on the other hand, reduced the regime to a state of shock and distrust. Bani-Sadr would write that Khomeini has said all those people who were arrested should be executed and many were executed at once, but then because of the war starting he claimed he got pardons for the rest from Khomeini. When the coup d'etat was discovered, the commanding officers of Khouzestan Army (brigades 92) were rubbed out!"[10]

After the war began, Khomeini's regime released about 170 pilots who had been purged or imprisoned when the coup d'etat was known. During October of the same year, another 600 pilots were released from prison. A few high ranking officers who were royalist along with another 100 ground force officers were also released from prison.[11]

As a result of the highly disorganized armed forces in Iran, the Iraqi forces achieved a great victory. During a few hours in the morning of September 23, Iraqi tanks progressed over 10 kilometers inside Iran, and also over 12 airports and air bases were bombed. The oil terminal of Khark Island and other military and economic targets were bombed. But the rapid progress of Iraq in the first day of the war faced numerous problems. There are two analyses of Iraq's attack:

1/Saddam Hussein wanted to take over Khuzestan in classic military terms, ruin the oil refinery and oil wells and to cut off this province from the rest of the country.[12]

2/According to the Revolutionary Council of Iraq's statement, the purpose of the attack was to overthrow Khomeini's regime. If that was their real reason for attacking Iran, the Iraqis were very short-sighted because without overtaking the capital, it is impossible to over-throw a government.[13] Besides, from a tactical viewpoint, the Iraqi forces were not able to reach Tehran. In any case, whatever was the true objective of Saddam Hussein, it was not achieved. After the fourth day of war, the remains of the armed forces and unarmed patriotism of the masses together halted the progress of the Iraqi forces.

In this respect, the Israeli government—despite the anti-Israeli position of Khomeini—supported Iran against Iraq. Without doubt Israel wanted the fall of Khomeini but it did not want Iraq to win the war. One week after the start of the war, General Mordecai Zippori, the vice Minister of the Israeli defense ministry said that Israel might deliver arms, Gabriel missiles and other US-made weapons to Iran.[14]

In October 1980, Moshe Dayan, the Israel foreign affairs minister, said that if US-made arms were not delivered to Iran, Iraq would win the war. This statement was perceived with considerations among the Western governments.[15] In this respect, Israel was not happy with Jordanian cooperation with Iraq against Iran, and Israel showed her desire that Iran not lose the war.

In October, the war between Iran and Iraq continued at full speed, and Iraq took over Khorramshahr on October 13. But the Iranian Air Force and Navy brutally damaged the Iraq forces when in the beginning of October, the Iranian Navy bombed all the Iraqi oil terminals in the Persian Gulf which brought Iraq's oil exports to a stand-still. On October 14, the Iranian Air Force struck Baghdad with pilots recently released from prison who flew in low altitude to be invisible to Iraqi radar. The Iraqi armed forces could not use Dayan's tactic which he employed in the 1967 War with Egypt. They wanted to eradicate the total air force without a doubt the rapid aid of Israel played a significant role in the re-inforcement of Iran's air forces.

Newsweek magazine in early November 1980 reported that Israel had secretly sold various arms and parts to Iran to be used against Iraq. Most of these arms were shipped to Iran via Holland.[16] Ahmad Heidari, an Iranian arms dealer in a hostage episode in 1981, in an interview with Le Monde, said he had been in charge of an arms deal for Iran and said on October 24, 1980 a few Scorpion tanks and 250 tires for F-4 jets were flown by Boeing 747 to Iran. Heidari was Beheshti's representative (Beheshti being an influential clergyman who died in an explosion in 1981), and indicated that 80% of arms were from Israel.[17]

A member of the French secret service agency, D.G.S.E., prepared a report about Iran-Israel relations which was eventually reported in the press. According to this report, the Iranian embassy in Paris was in the process of negotiation with Israeli representatives to buy parts for Phantom jets. Most of the negotiations were held in the Swiss Embassy because they were mediating the deal.

Pierre Pean, a French journalist, reported that the Israeli military attache in Paris told Ahmad Haydari, who was in charge of the arms deal on behalf of the Islamic Republic, that the Israelis were ready to give any parts and US-made arms which were needed by Iran on one condition, that there was a direct relation with the Islamic Republic, and that the agreement was written-up on the official letter-head of the Islamic Republic.[18]

There are other reports which indicate the rate of military aid and logistic aid which Israel gave Iran. The French TV reporter, Gerard Beaufils of Luxembourg RTL, who had been at the front when the war broke out between Iraq and Iran and was accused of treason by the revolutionary Pasdaran, arrested and imprisoned, wrote that in 1980, 350 Israeli technicians were working at Iranian airbases for the operation of F-4, F-5 and F-14's as well as training local specialists.[19]

Apparently, Many Israeli military advisors and technicians went to Iran based on bilateral agreements. There were secret meetings between Colonel Zarabi, the director of the Iranian military-industrial complex, and Colonel Ben-Youssef, an Israeli, in Zurich. The agenda of the meeting included training Iranian technicians to repair and alter war planes in order to be able to use Israeli-made parts. Iranian war planes were similar to Israeli, all made in the US, but were altered so that Israeli-made bombs could be fitted to them. After these modifications and the training period, the flood of Israeli arms began and a few Israeli military advisors secretly went to Iran to see the front and evaluate the situation.[20]

An Iranian officer, First-Lieutenant Mohammad-Reza Aminizadeh, chief of the first battalion of air ground forces, ran away in 1985 and applied for political asylum in England. In an interview with the Arabic magazine, Al-Dastur printed in London, he described his observations of the first contacts of Khomeini's regime with Israel. He also confirmed the trip of an Israeli mission early 1980 to Tehran and October 1980, one month after the war broke out, another went to Tehran via Istanbul. The chief of the Israel mission was Colonel Uri, a high-ranking army officer. Aminizadeh said "when he reached Tehran I guided him with a helicopter to Lavisan garrison. After five days in Tehran he had met most of the high ranking officials of the Islamic Republic even while the American diplomats were still hostage in Tehran. Three days after the mission returned to Tel Aviv one airline cargo flew to Larnaca and brought Phantom or F-14 parts, 'Tom Cat,' and since then the relations developed so much that besides arms, medicine, chicken, eggs and foodstuffs were also exported to Iran".[21]

The Israelis, in sending parts and arms to Iran acted so secretly and speedily so that officials in Carter's administration were shocked. Brezinski, head of the National Security Council under Carter, wrote "in the beginning of the war, Iran needed the US-made parts very badly. We tried to use their needs as a means of forcing Iran to release the hostages as soon as possible. In the middle of October, we had even thought of transferring some parts to Germany, Algeria, and Pakistan so that the Iranians could bring them with their own planes to Iran. It was exactly at this stage that we received news that the Israelis had secretly provided parts to Iran and had not paid any attention to the negative impact of this action for our influence on Iran for the sake of the hostages' release. Ed Muskie and I discussed this problem in detail and decided to recommend that the Secretary of State protest harshly to the Israelis because it was obvious that their action had damaged our very delicate process. To my knowledge, what we did was to deprive Israel for a short period of time by not giving them US-made weapons parts."[22]

However, the first cooperation between Israel and the Islamic Republic cannot ignore the Israeli bombing of the Iraqi nuclear installation Tuvatieh, called Tamuz by the Iraqis. A few days after the Iraqi attack, General Yehoshua Saguy, the chief of Israeli military intelligence, said on television that Israel was worried about Iraq's atomic reactor which was about to be completed. Not many days later, on September 30, 1981, while the war in Khuzestan was raging, an unknown plane dropped a bomb on the Iraqi reactor. Immediately, Iran claimed its air force had dropped the bomb but the Iraqis stated that the Israeli Air Force was responsible. According to the Iraqis, "the precision of the bombardment was such that according to the military commentator, this could not have been the work of Iranian pilots. The bomb hit its target but the curved cement wall of the reactor protected it from destruction. It is important to consider that in this region, only Iran and Israel had Phantoms and could do this kind of bombing.[23] The Israeli armed forces had tried on several occasions to stop the development of the Iraqi atomic reactor which was based on nuclear cooperation with France; a few months later, on June 7, 1981, the Israelis bombarded the station and officially claimed responsibility. This story is a very complex one and requires another chapter to fully explain events.

Note: It has been reported that Iran provided Israel with plans of the reactor and valuable information which assisted Israel in achieving its target of bombardment.

NOTICE: There were two attacks on the Iraqi reactor. One in 1980 (which was a minor attack) and one major attack in 1981.

1. *Sunday Times,* July 29, 1981
2. *New York Times,* December 18, 1986
3. *Islamic Revolution,* Tehran, May 25, 1981
4. Abol-Hassan Bani-Sadr, *L'Esperance trahie,* Papyrus, Paris, 1982, p. 179
5. Ibid
6. Ibid
7. Walter de Bock and Jean-Charles Deniau, *Des Armes pour l'Iran,* Gallimard, Paris, 1988, p. 20
8. Ibid, p. 20
9. *Middle East Contemporary Survey* (Volume Four, 1979-80), Holmes and Merer Publishers, Inc. N.Y. 1981, p. 471
10. Bani-Sadr, op. cit., p. 175-5
11. De Bock and Deniau, op. cit., p. 24
12. Claudia Wright, "Implications of the Iran-Iraq War," *Foreign Affairs,* Winter 1980-81, p. 286
13. De Bock and Deniau, op. cit., p. 26
14. *Le Monde,* March 26, 1982
15. De Bock and Deniau, op. cit., p. 29
16. *Iran Azad,* Paris, October 4, 1980
17. *Le Monde,* op. cit.
18. Pierre Pean, *La Menace,* Fayard, Paris, 1987, p. 22
19. Gerard Beaufils, *Tous Otages de Khomeini,* Garamont Archimbaud, Paris, 1987, p. 126
20. Pean, op. cit., p. 26-27

21. Al Dastur, London
22. Zbigniew Brezinski, *Power and Principle,* McGraw-Hill, 1983, p. 504
23. Charles Saint-Prot, “La Guerre de Golfe”, *Proche-Orient et Tiers Monde* No. 8, September 1983, p. 103

6

TEL AVIV-TEHRAN RELATIONS

1981 was a very important year in the relationship between the Khomeini Regime and Israel.

For the first time, the rate of arms dealing between Israel and Iran reached a level that Israel delivered arms to Iran, routed from Tel Aviv via Larnaca to Tehran. For the first time, the fate of Iraq-Iran War and the Ayatollah's regime was in the hands of Israel. Then suddenly, the secret relations between Israel and Iran became publicized and the Ayatollah learned some lessons in geopolitics and geostrategy and understood the shared fate of Iran and Israel. In the same year, Khomeini personally agreed to the arms purchases, and to political and military discussions with Israel.

In early 1981, Alexander Haig, the US Secretary of State after discussions with Robert MacFarlane and David Kimche of the Israeli Ministry of Foreign Affairs, decided to give the go-ahead to the Israeli government to export US-made parts to Iran.[1] In this way, the secret arms deal between Israel and Iran apparently became authorized by the US. On January 5th, 1981, Iranian forces attacked Iraq in the Susangerd region but failed to rout the Iraqis.[2] However, the first Iranian forces penetrated up to the central line of Iraq and progressed up to Hoveyzeh, but were surrounded by Iraqi forces on three sides. This attack was planned very badly in the first place. Bani Sadr was the commander-in-chief. The clergy criticized Bani Sadr for mismanagement and lack of efficiency, while on the other hand, Bani Sadr wanted to attract public opinion to the war fronts and away from the American hostages which is why he started the attack without adequate preparation.[3]

After the Susangerd attack failed, Iranian forces were not able to achieve any victory for a while. Finally, Bani Sadr, the President and commander-in-chief was forced out of office in June, 1981. He fled to Paris on July 29, 1981. Beside the internal conflict, one of the major reason for the weaknesses of the Khomeini Regime's military campaigns against Iraq was the lack of ammunition, parts and military equipment. Bani Sadr himself would write "Continuing the war is impossible without weapons, and changing our strategy against the world powers. The regime continuously propagates that during the Shah period, Iran had become the largest arsenal in the world. Strange stories occasionally appeared in the press, i.e. it was said that Iraqi planes bombed special targets inside Iran again and again which attracted Pasdar there to investigate and who discovered 50 Phantom planes stored underground, or another story which claimed that 500 artillery pieces were discovered in Kerman and that in Shiraz, missiles were found which could erase Iraq from the face of the Earth. All of these stories were fabricated and even Khomeini himself couldn't believe that Iran didn't have arms."[4]

On June 7, 1981, Israeli planes bombed the Iraqi atomic center near Baghdad which had already been bombed in suspicious ways on September 30, 1980. After the bombing, the Baghdad press and the international media discussed for the first time the Iran-Israel relationship against Iraq. June 5th was the anniversary of the Six-Day-War and a Jewish holiday. At 4:40 p.m., eight US-made F-16s with five F-15s escorting them set off from Etzioni airbase in the east of Sinai, flew over Jordan and reached Iraqi airspace, and fifty minutes later were above the Osirak Atomic Research Center. The Israeli planes dropped all their bombs and totally destroyed the $1.5 billion installation and the Iraqi-French Atomic Research Agreement went up in clouds of smoke.

The next day, Menachem Begin said that two sources had suggested different dates for this attack. One was in June 1981 and the other was in September, but the Israelis had discovered that the Iraqi Atomic Center would be operational before September and then they could not bomb because the radio-activity would have made life impossible in Baghdad and would have killed many innocent people.

The Israelis called this operation a legitimate defense and Menachem Begin at the end of July said in an election campaign speech that: "we will never allow the massacre of the Jews to be repeated. Baghdad was making herself ready to produce an atomic bomb and the Israeli government decided to waste no more time to ensure the safety of the Israeli people by halting the process."[5] Of course, Saddam Hussein had already publicly declared Iraq's desire to build an atomic reactor, but he denied Israeli propaganda which suggested that Iraq might use the bomb against Iran. In an interview with Al Thawra in Baghdad, he had said he wanted to assure the Iranian people that: "I do not intend to use the atomic bomb against them. The Iraqi objective was to have atomic power to use against the Zionists, our mutual enemies." For the Israelis, this sentence was enough to justify their attack. On June 23rd, Saddam Hussein said in a cabinet meeting that: "those countries which want peace and security in the region must help the Arab countries to have access to atomic power until they can face Israel which has atomic power. Sooner or later the Tamuz Reactor Center will be built and there is no force which can halt our access to atomic power.[6] During the bombing of the Osirak Center, one French technician was killed. The U.N. Security Council on July 19th condemned the Israeli action.[7]

Without doubt the Israeli decision to attack the Iraqi reactor was in response to the vulnerability of the Iraqi defense, particularly of the air force, because the major part of this force was involved in the war with Iran. Iraq had never been so vulnerable. On the other hand, the Israelis had superior power to the Iraqis anyway. Thus, Saddam was not in a position to react harshly against Israel.[8] There was also information that the Tamuz bombing was aided by aerial photographs supplied by Iran.[9]

The bombing gave Saddam a further excuse to propagandize against Iran and its relationship with Israel against the Arabs and Palestinians. The rapid reaction and embarassment in Iran against these accusations indicated how much the Khomeini Regime was vulnerable. Hashemi-Rafsanjani on June 9th said in the Majles "the Zionist and Imperialist propaganda machines have already so poisoned minds against the Islamic Republic that it is now impossible to change world opinion. The question we have to ask is about this important piece of news is why hadn't the Israelis attacked earlier? Once we bombed this reactor but the credit was given to Israel."

Rafsanjani claimed that the US, France and Israel had cooperated in building the reactor for Baghdad, but became disappointed with Saddam and were frightened that Iraqi Muslims might take over its control and made a pact with Saddam to destroy it. Rafsanjani suggested that the Iraqi forces had deliberately not tried to defend their air-space. He said if the Iraqis and other Arab planes had wanted to invade Israel, they all know that Iranian planes could do the job faster. He accused Hossein of being a big liar and the mass media of the Arab world as unworthy because of their lying and false accusations. "Nobody would believe that there is any greater enemy of Israel than the Islamic Republic. Despite the fact that we are still at war, the Military High Command Council decided to release Iraqi prisoners of war so that they could return to fight against Israel, and our revolutionary guards have said they are ready to fight with Israel. This is not propaganda but the truth. Don't confuse our people!!"[10]

Regarding all the claims previously mentioned, Khomeini's regime was still working hard to neutralize public opinion inside and outside Iran about the accusations of cooperation with Israel. Another episode without doubt would uncover the curtain of secrecy over the extensive military cooperation between Iran and Israel. The Iranian political situation during the ousting of Bani-Sadr and the taking-over of the entire control of the armed forces and the continuation of war by Ayatollah Khomeini and his trusted cronies brought the government much closer together. According to the report by **Le Canard Enchaine** on June 13, 1984, the value of the arms deal with Israel since 1981 was over $500 million. Most of these arms purchased were spare parts and ammunition which were directly purchased from Israel. The arms transaction was approved by Khomeini himself.

On July 18, 1981, a piece of news suddenly became the headline of all international press, the so-called "November Tango." The story was about an Argentinian charter plane, CL44, that had carried US-made arms and Israeli ammunition to Tehran. On return from Tehran, the plane flew over Russian aerospace and was shot down. The Jerusalem Post first wrote the story on July 23, 1981. Then, it reached the headlines of the European and American papers. A little prior to this incident, Colonel Kuchek-Deghan, the deputy-chief of Logistic Armed Forces signed an agreement with Yaacov Nimrodi, who was an Israeli Colonel, for the purchase of $135 million worth of ammunition from Israel, and included in this shopping list were Lance ground-to-ground missiles, Hawk ground-to-air missiles, 155 millimeter copperhead mortar-shells, etc."[11]

The purchase of arms was not the main problem of the Khomeini Regime; carrying the arms to Iran was the most difficult task. In the early spring of 1980, the Iranian government was looking for a transportation agency that could carry 360 tons of parts, tanks and ammunitions from Israel to Iran.[12]

Finally, two individuals, a Swiss and a Briton known as Andreas Jenni and McCafferty, not well-known in the field of arms smuggling, became very interested in the deal. They signed an agreement with Khomeini's agent in London under the name of Cover Firm Company, whose headquarters was in Tel Aviv. The agreement reads as follows: "All the purchased arms should be carried out to Tehran via Larnaca in 12 flights.[13] The value of these cargoes are $27.9 million.[14] According to the agreement, $600,000 was to be paid cash in advance to McCafferty. He leased a cargo plane from Transporte Aero Rioplatens Co. in Buenos Aires which was called "November Tango."[15] On July 10, that plane flight document was changed. A Cypriot agent said later according to the existing document: "November Tango" carried 6750 kilograms of pipe to be carried to Tehran.[16]

After the plane crashed an official at Larnaca airport said that "November Tango" had stopped there four times en route from Tel Aviv to Tehran.[17] On July 18, "November Tango" crashed on the way back from Tehran in Soviet Armenestan, apparently because near Yerevan in Turkey it flew into Soviet air-space. The Larnaca control detected two shining spots on the monitor, meaning two planes, crash into each other. November Tango disappeared. There are two stories about this even. One says that the plane was hit by a MIG 25.[18] The other report from Tass indicated that the plane appeared out of control, flew into Soviet airspace and didn't pay any attention to the airport controller, hit another plane in the air and crashed.[19]

Of course,the Tass report contradicts Jenni's statement which claimed that Larnaca was dangerous and full of spies.[20] It is certain that the Russians had discovered through their spy network about the Iranian purchase of the US-made arms through the Israelis and they wanted to warn Iran by crashing "November Tango" that such Iranian action was not acceptable. Israeli officials said that the Soviet message to Iran could be read in this way, that the European countries, Soviet Union and North Korea could supply Iran with arms but not Israel nor the US.[21]

Iranian and Israeli officials immediately denied any connection between the crash and any arms deals. However the Israeli denial was not very serious and then they kept silent.[22] The Khomeini Regime officials were very nervous and said that the whole story was fabricated and the press reports were a plot against the Revolution by social imperialism.[23]

On August 24, 1981, Khomeini in a speech to Muslim students from India and Pakistan who were touring Iran, denied any connection with the Israeli government and said: "from the beginning we were against the condemned Zionist tribe. Prior to this revolution, the Pahlavi regime was constantly connected with the corrupt Israeli government and this is why we were always opposed to Pahlavi. Now they accuse us of buying arms from Israel. If we don't regard them as human, how could we deal with them? Now, it is over 30 years that wherever we spoke or distributed communiques, one of our major topics was the cruelty of Israel but no Arab leader ever cooperated with us to face Israel."

In the same speech, he also mentioned the bombing of the Iraqi atomic reactor by Israel: "it is said now that Saddam to rescue himself from the failed invasion of Iran now brought Israel into the war, and they bombarded the atomic center so that everyone believes that Israel is against Saddam and the Baathist government. They find excuses that Israel has a connection with Iran. This is a childish statement and absolutely false. They pretend that an Islamic country like Iran could be a supporter of Israel. When we started this movement, one of our major issues was to eradicate Israel from the earth. How come they want to prove that we are the supporters of Israel? Please brothers, see with your own eyes if we are fighting with Israeli arms or with the arms of fate."[24] The Iraqis took advantage of the crash of "November Tango" against Israel and Iran. They called officials from the US Interests Office in Baghdad and protested that the delivery of more arms to Israel would create a surplus of arms which would allow Israel to sell to Iran.[25] The Iraqis officially informed all the Arab governments that Israel was selling US-made spare parts and arms to Iran, which was impossible without US support.[26]

In contrast to this, the Khomeini Regime was annoyed at the publicity, this case had received outside Iran while inside Iran public opinion was shocked by Khomeini's contradictory position. The Khomeini Regime claimed that the entire story was untrue and at the end of August, the Syrian Ambassador and the PLO mission in Tehran were interviewed by Iranian radio and television and officially supported the position of Iran and denied any arms purchases.

Later the PLO in an official communique, denied the statement of their mission in Tehran and said that was not the official PLO position in the matter. Ebrahim Suss, the PLO Mission head in Paris, in a French television interview said: "Regarding the Islamic Republic as a supporter of Palestinians, we also support the struggles of the Iranian people for democracy and freedom."

Following the PLO statement about the Tehran-Tel Aviv connection, Hani-al Hassan, the first Palestinian Ambassador to revolutionary Iran and personal emissary of Yasser Arafat, met Massoud Rajavi, the leader of the Mojaheddin Khalgh, in Paris and emphasized the PLO support of the Mojaheddin. The Islamic Republic's propaganda machine kept silent about this.

Finally, Khomeini, in order to deceive the public decided to attack Israel and deny any relation between his regime and Israel. On 6th September, 1981, in a message for the Hajj ceremonies, he told the pilgrims again and again that the imperialist propaganda horn of accusations claimed we had relations with Israel to purchase arms in the hope of separating us from the Arabs and creating hostility among Muslims to pave the way for super-power domination in this region. Everybody knows that Iran is a serious enemy of Israel and one of the major conflicts with the deposed Shah was his friendly relation with Israel. It is over twenty years that we have in all our speeches and communiques compared Israel to the United States as an invader and usurper. In all the demonstrations of the Islamic Republic, we accuse Israel as well as the US as enemies of our country and we have decided not to sell them oil. This ridiculous claim about relations with Israel was created by the propaganda machine of the US, the illegitimate mother of Israel and the little brother of Begin, in order to create disunity among Iranians and Arabs. All Muslims, especially all Arabs, must know that the issue is not Iranian relations with Israel, but the essential problem is imperialism between East and West, because Islam can unite all the Muslims of the world under the flag of unity and consequently, cut the hands of the tyrant imperialists from the Islamic lands. Today, Sadat, with a mass arrest of Muslim brothers in Egypt, has completed his service to Israel. His alliance with the US and particularly with Israel has ruined Arab national prestige. Despite all Israeli crimes against the Palestinians, Israel has recently started excavations in Al-Aksa which was the altar of the Muslims and wants to ruin it.[27]

But the propaganda and disinformation of Khomeini did not help him. After the crash of the Argentinian plane, one Israeli official stated that the relationship between Israel and Iran existed because of a shared enemy, Iraq. He added "one of the major reasons for cooperation between the two countries is the likely access of Iraq to the atomic bomb and its unconditional support for PLO and Baghdad's propaganda and diplomatic activities against Israel. Iraq is our first enemy, "The source added that Iraq's propaganda vis a vis the Iran-Iraq war would ultimately benefit Israel, and the Iranian government was pleased about Israeli support for Shiites in South Lebanon. The Lebanese Phalange who are Christian and allied with Israel, also support the Shiite Muslims.[28]

The Jerusalem Post in regard to the story of "November Tango," referred to an official report that the military and information relation between Iran and Israel after the fall of the Shah has continued; and only for a short time during the revolution it was discontinued.[29]

As a result of the arms embargo by US, the Islamic Republic had no choice except to buy its needed arms from the black market paying high prices. When Israel offered arms to Iran at prices much lower than the black market prices, Iran grabbed the opportunity.[30] Khomeini in contrast to the general perception would take advantage of any opportunity for re-enforcing his position; he found out quickly during the US hostage period and the climax of war with Iraq that he could keep the army busy on the front and use the war as an excuse for extending the life of his regime. In order to control all the crisis he was facing at home and abroad, he discovered that the best policy for his government was not to have a policy, particularly foreign policy.

However, Khomeini decided to have secret relations with Israel. Israel itself, was suffering from an economic crisis, especially in foreign exchange. By selling arms and US-made spare parts with a lucrative profit, Israel solved her foreign exchange shortages problem extensively.

The Jerusalem Post reported that US sources analysis from Israeli sources believed that the Khomeini Regime would fall very soon. They had to keep their logistic connection with armed forces, in order to purchase Iranian oil for Israel. It was rather strange that after this statement, over ten Iranian officials were terrorized and a number of bomb explosions occured in different parts of Tehran.[31]

From the fall of 1981, both Iran and Israel for their own strategic interests became very active, i.e. the Israelis on December 14, 1981, joined the Golan Heights de facto to Israel and at the same time, the residential areas of Beirut and the Palestinian bases were bombed. On the other hand, Khomeini, having access to Israeli arms, achieved extraordinary victories in bombing the Iraqi oil installations, breaking the surrender of Abadan, and pushing Iraqi forces out of Khorramshar. In September, in a big campaign called "On the Road to Qods," in the vicinity of Bostan, Iranian forces regained all the territories surrounding Qasre-Shirin, and by December, they had been able to weaken the position of Arab countries in the region. In October 1981, Kuwait was attacked and in December, Iran decided to arrange a coup-d'etat in Bahrain, which failed.

The biggest military victory of the Khomeini Regime in 1981 was the re-taking of occupied lands in Bostan, thanks to the arms purchased from Israel. It is interesting to know that Ayatollah Khomeini named this operation: "The Road to Jerusalem."

1. *Washington Post,* November 29, 1986
2. Anthony Cordesman, *The Iran-Iraq War and Western Security 1984-1987,* Jane's, London, 1987, p. 15
3. Stephan R. Grummon, *The Iran-Iraq War: Islam Embattled.* Georgetown University, Washington, D.C. 1982, p. 26
4. Abolhassan Bani-Sadr, *L'Esprance Trahie,* Papyrus, Paris 1982, pp. 183, 398
5. Pierre Pean, *La Menace,* Fayard, Paris, 1987, p. 102
6. Ibid. p. 101-2
7. Charles Saint-Prot, "La Guerre du Golfe", *Proche-Orient et Tiers Monde* No. 8, September 1983, p. 110
8. Grummon, op. cit., p. 52
9. *Sunday Telegraph,* London, June 14, 1981
10. Ali-Akbar Hashemi-Rafsanjani, *Notghaye Pish as Dastur Majles Shoraye Eslami:* Ravabete Umumi Majles Shoraye Eslami, Tehran, 1362, pp. 120-121

11. Pean, op. cit., pp. 23-24
12. *Sunday Times,* July 26, 1981
13. *Middle East Perspective,* New York, October 1981
14. *Boston Globe,* July 17, 1981
15. *Sunday Times, op. cit.*
16. *The Times,* July 27, 1981
17. Scott Armstrong et al., *The Chronology (The Documented Day-by-Day Account of the Secret Military Assistance to Iran and the Contras,* Warner Books, New York, 1987, p. 8
18. *Jerusalem Post,* July 28, 1981
19. *Sunday Times,* op. cit.
20. *Sunday Times,* op. cit.
21. *Christian Science Monitor,* August 6, 1981
22. *New York Times,* August 24, 1981
23. *Jerusalem Post,* July 27, 1981
24. *Peyamha va Sokhanranihaye Imam Khomeini Dar Shesh Mahe Avval Sal 1360,* Entesharate Nuri, Tehran, 1360, p. 366-367
25. *Christian Science Monitor,* August 8, 1981
26. *Jerusalem Post,* August 2, 1981
27. *Peyamha,* op. cit., pp. 399-400
28. *Christian Science Monitor,* August 6, 1981
29. *Jerusalem Post,* August 2, 1981
30. *Middle East Perspective,* October 1981
31. Ibid

7

TEHRAN-TEL AVIV RELATIONS REINFORCED (1982-1983)

From the beginning of 1982, information-sharing and military relations were extended between Iran and Israel. One of the special characteristics of this period was that the Western press verified the information about the growing relationship between Iran and Israel. Israeli and Iranian leaders began to take advantage of their friendly cooperation internally and internationally, although the Israelis always tried to hide this relationship especially in early 1982 when they talked about helping the army, not the Khomeini Regime. On February 8th, 1982, Panorama, a BBC television program, broadcast a major interview with David Kimche, the head of Israeli Foreign Affairs and the former associate director of Mossad, Lubrani, the former Israeli Ambassador in Tehran, and Yaakov Nimroodi, the former Israeli military attache in Tehran. Kimche talked about equipping the Iranian army and the necessity of keeping the Iranian army powerful. Lubrani said it was necessary to organize a military coup against Khomeini and said that with one hundred tanks it would be possible to take-over Tehran without incurring more than 10,000 deaths. He clarified that Israel intended that this coup d'etat would occur as quickly as possible but the US had always postponed the process while it made decisions.[1]

Without doubt, the Israeli experts were not unaware that most of the arms and equipment, except the airplane spare parts, that they were delivering to Iran would all go directly to the revolutionary Pasdaran and security forces of the Ayatollah, and the result would be the weakening of the army and increasing competition between the army and increasing competition between the army and the Pasdaran. However, they were not aware of any coup plot made jointly by the Israelis and Americans, and Lubrani's claim was not supported by any other source. On the other hand, it is very hard to imagine that Khomeini's regime in those critical days could have survived without Israeli support. It is very illogical that on the one hand, the Israelis were providing weapons to the army while on the other hand, they were busy announcing to the world that a coup was about to happen. What can be understood from the Israeli activities in Iran was that they were covering up their major military and strategic objectives in the region and creating fear among the Arab countries by propagating support for the Iranian army while behind the curtain they were helping Khomeini's government. In fact, it was very obvious that they were not in the business of plotting against Khomeini.

Various reports provided by US information agencies during 1984-1985 indicated that the Israelis were always in close contact with Iran. When these reports were later published, they revealed that Israel not only provided US-made spare parts and arms, it facilitated directly to provide more US-made arms from private sources for the Khomeini Regime from 1982. MacFarlane, the former national security cheif, said in a joint meeting of the Senate and Congressional investigation committee that the CIA had not provided any reports about Iran and Israeli arms deals between 1981 and 1985. He also claims that a few times he had asked the CIA Chief to verify the Iran-Israeli arms deal, but the CIA Chief had responded that this was rumor. Nevertheless, McFarlane in a telegraph to Schultz reported there was no doubt that Israel had been in very close contact with Iran for a long time.[2]

In order to prove the military relationship of Israel with Iran, there is no need to consider American official statements about the story of Iran and Israeli relation; because every one of them tries to take advantage of Iranian affairs for their own purpose. There are numerous non-official reports about the affairs. Washington Post, in May 1982, reported that Israel secretly sold arms to Iran to use in the war against Iraq. In this report, it was reported that General Haig, the former US Secretary of State, not only did not prohibit Israel, but actually persuaded them to support Iran and thanked them for their efforts.[3]

The International Herald Tribune reported that for a long

time Iran had been able to get the necessary arms from Israel.[4] One of the major aspects of military cooperation between Israel and the Khomeini Regime which has not been considered so far, was the assistance of Israeli intelligence and military service to Iran for access to the international arms market for other kinds of weapons compatible with US-made arms. This action, apart from its military importance, could in fact be a cover for secrecy and making the whole process much more complex and secret from the public inside Iran, especially after the publicity of the November Tango affairs in July 1981. A serious secret cover-up was to develop between Iran and Israel. The major reason was the indirect assistance of Israel, based on Iran's need after the 1979 revolution. Even the Iranian army did not know what arms and spare parts they had in stock because in the hey-day of the revolution, the revolutionary pasdars has smashed the military computers which held the records of all the military spare parts and the stock number of the weapons. They thought these computers were connected to the CIA and Pentagon.[5] One Iranian news reporter who was in Iran during February 1981 said he was a witness when the revolutionary pasdars with machine guns shot out all the military computers in the Ministry of War.[6]

During 1981, the logistical communication center of Israel and Iran was in London. The officials of the Khomeini Regime's embassy in London used to give a list of spare parts and arms secretly to the information officers of Israeli embassy. After a few days, they gave a list of governments, companies and those people who had the parts or were ready to sell to Iran via Khomeini's contacts in London. These secret person-to-person communications required no telex between Tel Aviv and Tehran and left no computer record of official document.[7]

During 1983, an anti-Khomeini paper in Paris got access to some documents on the cooperation between Israel and the Khomeini Regime. A letter from the Israeli army to the purchase office of the Iranian Air Force in London was printed in the paper. The content of the print-out indicated the kind, the place of make, the place of sale and the dealer of spare parts which were all clearly coded on a computer sheet.[8]

Although Shimon Perez, the Israeli Prime Minister, was assuring the United States that there were no arms deal between Israel and Iran,[9] and Iranian offficials were attacking Israel in their media, saying that Israel is the devil of Zionism, the

Israeli military aid to Iran not only prevented the total collapse of the Iranian forces, but also helped support a heavy Iranian attack against the Iraqi army during 1982. On March 28, 1982, the Khomeini Regime in an attack called "Fath ul mobin," in the western front between Dezful and the northern part of the Alemareh gained a great victory and regained a large part of Iran which was occupied by the Iraqi forces.[10] But the Iranians who had enough human resources and whose army had been re-equipped with Israeli arms refused to accept the cease fire. Again, in April, the Iranian forces in major attack recaptured the remaining part of Iran occupied by Iraq and pushed the Iraqi forces away from Almareh. During May 3 to May 11, the great Iranian attack in the province of Khouzestan continued and eventually Iranian forces reached the Iraqi border. On May 24, the Iranian army regained Khorramshahr, putting Iraqi forces on the defensive. These victories one after another would have not been possible without Israeli military help. The military aid by Isreal was estimated at about $250 million.[11] In other words, Iran, without Israeli help, could not achieve any victory. Time magazine reported in November 1982 that Israel had sold Iran a Tow missile through their middleman, Firuz Azzizy who was living in Athens. According to available records, these missiles were first shipped via Amsterdam to Iran.[12]

In May 1982, General Ariel Sharon, the Israeli Defense Minister, went on a trip to the US and during his trip, a few reports about arms sales to Iran were published in the papers. In response to the media reports, a State Department spokesman said that the United States was not aware of any such arms deals to Iran. But Sharon formally announced that the sale of arms deal was with the knowledge of the United States. Then, Sharon explained that the Israeli arms were delivered via a third country and the complete list of the arms deals was available for US officials.

Sharon's statement had a drastic backlash for the Ayatollah's anti-Zionist prestige. It was exactly during the climax of Khomeini's victory against Iraq and the rhetoric of Khomeini's speech was that after the taking of Karbala (one of the sacred places of the Shiites), it is the time of Jerusalem.

Sharon, in an interview with the press, stated clearly that arms sales to Iran were for strategic purposes and not for the support of the Ayatollah's Regime: "We have told American officials that every body knows that the Ayatollah is a dictator, but we have no other choice except to keep a window open toward Iran for the day the war would be over and somebody else would take over control in Iran; this does not mean that we are supporting the Ayatollah."[13]

Sharon, in his trip to Washington, said again; "Iraq is our real enemy. I hope diplomatic relations would be restored with Iran again." Sharon was trying to justify the sale of arms to Iran. Four months later, in an interview in Paris, he said: "Israel has a vital interest in the continuation of war in Persian Gulf and a victory for Iran." This was not only Sharon's view since Yitzhak Shamir, the Prime Minister from the Likud party, and Shimon Perez from the Labor party, both believed in the same thing.[14] When Sharon returned to Israel, he was harshly criticized by the Israeli parliament for revealing the secret of the arms deal to Iran. But the criticism of Sharon did not stop General Ralphael Eytan, the Chief staff of the Israeli army, who had sharply criticized the war between Iraq and Iran, from verifying that, because of Iran's successes in the war against Iraq, the probability of Iraq's invasion of Israel had become very remote. Then, he said: this war is to the benifit of Isreal. Eytan, in response to the question: "How come your country is ready to help the Islamic Republic which considers Israel its real enemy, and its final objective is to free occupied Palestine?", said: "if Iran decided to invade Israel, first her forces should cross Iraq and then, they should cross Jordon; in order to get to Israel they should destroy those two countries and when they reach Israel, they would realize that we are not Iraq nor Jordan and to overcome us would not be possible."[15]

In reaction to Sharon's interviews and other Israeli officials, the Khomeini Regime officials not only denied their comments but even called them totally false and baseless. Khomeini, in a broadcast speech, called the Israelis "unclean," and denied the purchase of arms from Israel. On the same day, Khamenehi, the President of Iran, said: "Iran had never purchased arms from Israel during the war of Iraq." He said: "We have never purchased arms from anybody." World public opinion still was not completely aware about the secret deals of Israel with Iran.

In June 1982, the strategic cooperation between Likud government and the Khomeini Regime came to the surface. When Iranian forces were gaining success in the front, Israel invaded Lebanon as if an invisible symphony orchestra was conducting harmonizing Iranian and Israeli military achievements in both

Iraq and Lebanon.

On June 4, 1982, Israeli planes bombed Beirut as retaliation to the assassination of their ambassador, Shlomo Argov, in London. Over 200 people were killed in Beirut. Two days later, the great invasion, the so-called Peace for Galilee started and Israeli forces from three directions attacked Lebanon. Fourteen thousand five hundred Palestinian guerillas in West Beirut were surrounded by Israeli troops. For the first time, television news around the world showed Yasser Arafat depressed and tired with Klashinkoff in his hand, and looking very thoughtful, walking on the campus of Beirut University. It was reported then that he had found a safe refuge in Russian Embassy.[16]

After the Israeli invasion to Lebanon, the Iraqi leader said he would retract all his forces from Iran and suggested for counter attack to Israel, to have a cease fire with Iran. But, Iran rejected the Iraqi proposal quickly and asked for continuation of the war. In July, for the first time Iranian forces in an attack, called "Ramazan," invaded Iraq, the purpose of the invasion was to take Basrah. In that operation, Iran did not achieve very much except some progress in north-eastern part of Basrah. But, the Iranian Air Force which was equipped with US-made aircrafts and has led to an increase in Israeli technicians helping in preparation for Iranian Air Force to invade the Iraqi cities, the war of cities between the two countries.[17] The effect and the coincidence of the Khomeini Regime forces invasion of Basrah and the Israeli attacks on Beirut was of considerable importance. For the first time, the Israeli army was able to overcome the capital of an Arab country. As a result, the Palestinian forces were in serious danger.

During the Israeli attack on Beirut in 1982 and the forcing of the Palestinians to evacuate Lebanon, Palestinian relations with Iran deteriorated very quickly and there was no sign of any alliance and friendship between Arafat and Khomeini.[18] Khomeini's threat to Iraq's sovereignty made Yasser Arafat so confused and perplexed that he ignored the serious danger which his forces were facing. During the summer of 1983, Arafat was busy trying to find an end to the Iran-Iraq war, commuting from Baghdad to Tehran, when suddenly Israeli tanks and soldiers entered Beirut.[19]

The Khomeini Regime reaction to the Israel invasion of Lebanon was very deceitful and full of lies. Iranian officials as usual denied the reports about arms purchases from Israel. Tavakoli, the labor minister of Khomeini's regime, in an interview with Le Matin, denied the rumors about the arms purchases from Israel and US. He said: "These talks try to weaken our anti-American position in the face of other nations."[20]

There was no end to Khomeini's demagoguery and after the Israeli invasion of Lebanon, the Khomeini Regime demanded a solidarity front from the Arab countries who were friendly to the Soviet position and Ayatollah himself said: "Israel should be overcome militarily." Exactly during that period one Israeli military mission was on the way to Iran via Ankara in order to re-emphasize and re-negotiate their military relations.[21] Khomeini's propaganda machine was saying he would support the progressive forces of Lebanon and the Palestinian forces to rebuff the Israeli forces. A diplomatic and military mission went to Damascus and suggested that Iran was ready to send military forces to the Lebanese front. It is important to mention that the Khomeini Regime media used to label Saddam Hossein an American puppet or athiest but suddenly they changed their labelling of Saddam to Zionist and later labelled Tarig Aziz, the Deputy Prime Minister, as a Jew and that his name was in fact Tarig Yuhanna Aziz.

Mir Hossein Mousavi, the Prime Minister of the Khomeini Regime, on June 9, officially said that the Cabinet in their last meeting had decided to establish a special fund for participating in the Lebanese war and to get the approval from the Majles.[22] In fact, the budget allocation was for a special fund for the purchase of arms from Israel to use it in the Gulf war. The Ayatollah was not able to do anything, except take a symbolic position. More than one thousand pasdars (revolutionary guards) went on a mission to Syria, but their presence in Syria was not a help but an embarrassment. First of all, their arms were not sufficient and their number was not considered a threat to Israel.[23] The skills of the revolutionary pasdars were not on a scale that could add to Khomeini's prestige. Some of those forces went to West Beirut. Reports from the front indicated that the majority of revolutionary guards would be killed in the front because they did not have enough training and skills.[24] Some other pasdars went with Syrian forces to the Rachmaya Chouf Heights, but they didn't fight and returned to Baalbec where the majority of people were Shiite.[25]

Hafez al Assad, the Syrian President, was quite aware of the danger of war with Israel and was very concerned about any involvement with Israel and also wanted to get rid of the Palestinians in Lebanon in order to reinforce his position in Lebanon. He made a secret deal with Iran about not sending any revolutionary pasdars to Lebanon. For the first time, Hashemi-Rafsanjani, in an interview with Iran radio, said: "When we sent forces to Syria, Hafez Assad said we have to send forces to our border with Iraq instead and later he added that without solving the problem with Iraq, the problem in Lebanon would not be resolved. Libya's leader said the same thing: "It is interesting that Ayatollah himself on June 21, changed his position against the Israeli invasion of Lebanon and expressed his view that he is opposed to sending forces to Lebanon." Then, he added: "the superpower conspiracy failed in the region and we were being deceived too. In order to divert our attention from our country, they arranged that Israel invade Lebanon. When they saw that Iran might be victorious in the war with Iraq and add Iraq to Iran and that the other small countries in the region might join us, they forced Begin to attack Lebanon. Their plot was that as Iran is very sensitive to Lebanon, all the Iranian forces would be involved with Israeli invasion of Lebanon. Consequently, Saddam would be saved. Today, if everybody pays attention to Lebanon, all preachers and speakers and writers, this will be a success for USA. Why? Because Iran would forget about the war with Iraq, and consequently, Iran would be the loser of both, Iraq and Lebanon. Therefore, we have to march to Lebanon via Iraq that is after taking-over Iraq, we can enter Beirut easily. Now, this is everybody's duty to uncover this plot throughout the country. After the victory on Iraq, we can go on to Lebanon. Do not let people forget about their war with Iraq.[26]

In early July, Israeli forces caught one of Khomeini's pasdars fighting in Lebanon. They showed him to a reporter. The pasdar in a TV interview said: he was an electrical technician from Javadieh in south Tehran. He explained to the reporter that in order to get an exit visa he was obliged to come to the war zone in Beirut. He also complained about the corruption in Iran and criticized the PLO commandos about how they had left their families behind after the Israeli invasion. The Israeli broadcast some parts of this pasdar's interview on the Persian language program of Radio Israel. Sending Iranian forces to Lebanon by Khomeini had become a disaster. Amal, the Lebanese militia, and the majority of the Lebanese Shiites were all unhappy about the presence of the Palestinians in their country. They all welcomed the presence of the Israelis. The Nouvel Observateur magazine in Paris wrote that 8,500 Shiites in the city of Davayer in the vicinity of Nabetiye welcomed Saad Haddad forces (an Israeli agent who led a band of Lebanese Christian armed men. He died in 1986). He took over one district with Israeli cooperation and called for a free Lebanon. Despite the fact that the Sherman tanks had pictures of the Virgin Mary on their sides, the Shiites kissed them and welcomed them to the area. There were posters of Khomeini and Khalkhali on the walls of the city and a slogan on canvas which carried Khomeini's message about fighting imperialism and Zionism. Among the welcomers of the Free Lebanon Army and the Israeli forces were the clergy of the city. Sheikh Hashem Ibrahim welcomed Major Haddad and said: "we have come out of hell's circle."[27] The Israeli army allowed the Christian Falange and the paramilitary to carry their arms in return for carrying out the duties of the Israeli army.[28]

The Israeli invasion of Lebanon concerned most international organizations, particularly the Arab League which paid very careful attention to the military and strategic cooperation between Tehran and Tel Aviv. As a result, numerous reports which pointed out how Israel had sold weapons confiscated from Palestinians in Lebanon to Khomeini Regime[29] and were used in the war front with Iraq. The Israelis charged Iran over $50 million dollars for this hardware. According to secret reports by the CIA on August 1982, in one arms deal with the Khomeini Regime, the Israelis received $50 million.This report indicated that most of the weaponry that Israel sold to Iran were taken from the PLO in Lebanon. However, the Tel Aviv government said it had only sold plane spare parts and tires to Iran in order to enable the Iranian Air Force to fly against Iraqi positions.[30] On August 20th, this news was published in the Washington Post and repeated in detail in the western press. All reports emphasized that cooperation between Tehran and Jerusalem had never stopped. Publicly, Tehran supported the Palestinian position at the time, and used the rhetoric that they were going via Karbala to take over Jerusalem. As a result of this cooperation, a profit of $50 million worth of arms from PLO went to Israel.[31]

In March 1982, the New York Times printed a series of documents which indicated that half of the total arms sold to Iran in the past eighteen months by Israel were alone worth over

$100 million.[32] According to the reports by the Jaffee Institute for Strategic Studies in Tel Aviv, Iran had purchased in the period from 1980 to 1983, over $500 million worth of arms from Israel.[33] Israel did not only provide arms for the war but also sold other kinds of equipment that could be used for internal security purposes, such as cracking down any internal opposition. The weekly magazine Panorama, printed in Italy, discovered one arms deal between Israel and Iran which involved 45,000 Uzi machine guns and various kinds of surveillance and security equipment.[34] Also, there were other reports about the delivery of Iranian oil to Israel. In August 1982, Iran sold oil at a 25% discount to Israel.[35]

Khomeini, after these documents were revealed, in order to deny his relation with Israel, used his ambassador at the United Nations to make a move in the direction of cancelling the membership of Israel in the United Nations. It was obvious that the Iranian proposal would not be accepted by the general council but international diplomatic circles and the press called the move of the Khomeini Regime a reaction against the Arab countries who did not cooperate, because three days prior to this expulsion motion Iraq had demanded a cease-fire in the Gulf war and a return of all forces within the international borders which had been approved 119 to 1, the Khomeini Regime solely against. While all the Arab countries supported the Iraqi move or abstained, Khomeini ordered Said Rajaii Khorassani, his U.N. emissary, to suggest the Israeli expulsion in order to put the Arabs in a deadlock. Finally, the Security Council rejected Iran's proposal and did not include it on its agenda.[36]

In September 1982, when the war between Palestinians and Israel on the one hand, and Iraq and Iranians on the other, was raging, the Israelis entered the western Muslim section of Beirut and achieved their objective. The Khomeini Regime, by the end of September in the operation called "Muslim Ibn Aqil" near Mandali and the southern border of Ghasr-Shirin, had gained a big victory. After this victory, the war objectives of the Ayatollah were the trial of Saddam Hossein, the eradication of the Baath Party, and the creation of an Iraqi Islamic Republic, plus total war damages. But, slowly, the Ayatollah's forces didn't progress any further after mid-winter, and the war almost came to a standstill on all fronts.[37]

Israel gained military and strategic advantages from the continuation of war between Iran and Iraq. In 1982, it gained a better tactical position out of the conflict which was changing from a war between Iran and Iraq into an inter-Arab struggle. However, Arab leaders recommended at Fez Summit of 1982 that Hafez Assad and Saddam Hossein put aside their conflicts and that Syria should avoid supporting Khomeini in order to force him to accept a cease-fire.

In the spring of 1983, the US State Department brought a plan called "Operation Staunch" in order to stop the export of arms from different countries to Iran. In fact, US officials protested to a few countries, such as Israel, for its arms sales to Iran and asked that this traffic be stopped. General Sharon said that the sale of arms to Iran had been stopped.[38] But Israeli officials' reports were always conflicting. Ovadia Sofer, the Israeli ambassador in France, in an interview with French Television in October 1983, said: "all the arms deals with Iran since the beginning of the war with Iraq were true and worth over $100 million." In fact, there is no reason for cutting the arms sales to Iran. It was quite obvious that Israel, by controlling the kind of arms sales and the secret military information was able to control the war. A number of times, Israeli officials stated that in this war, no-one wins or loses and even that there might not be an end to the war. General Aharon Yariv, the former commander of Israeli military intelligence, in a conference in the Tel Aviv University in 1986, said: "It will be excellent if the war between Iran and Iraq would end without a victory for either side. But, it would be even better if the war between them continues, otherwise, Iraq might organize an eastern front against Israel.[39]

From 1983 onward Iran showed some hints of rapprochement with the West, particularly the United States. In the beginning of the same year, Washington received some good news from Iran, that 240 members of the Tudeh party had been arrested and that the activities of the Russian Embassy had been curbed drastically.[40] On January 8, Ali Akbar Hashemi Rafsanjani, the Speaker of the House, was able to reinforce his position as the second man. In a speech about the United States, he said: "Come like a human being, behave and do business with our people, and see your goods as a human, then, we would behave as a human with you." Radio Israel in its Persian program had broadcasted the speech with a commentary that Rafsanjani's speech showed a positive shift toward the West.

Rafsanjani's statement about the conditions for starting relations with the West could not be stated without Khomeini's approval. It seemed that Khomeini, in order to solve the numerous problems that he was facing, had decided to liberalize in order to attract the trust of the middle class. His government sent a mission to the United Kingdom, France and the United States, in order to bring some of the technocrats, merchants and self-exiled professional back. Khomeini promised as long as there is Islam, there is business as usual. He blamed Bani-Sadr, the former President, for extremism.[41]

The tendency toward liberalism and the signal for starting relations with the US emerged when the war in the front did not progress further. A series of attacks by Khomeini forces, the so called "Alfadjar," to take Basreh, did not gain any victories, but they lost again and again. Iranians started to complain about the way Khomeini was handling the war and he was rapidly losing credibility.[42]

During February of 1983, Iran was ready to pay a $26 million penalty for US embassy which had been called the "Spy Nest." This payment was a symbolic act. It was mostly for the normalization of relations between Washington and Tehran. A series of discussions started about the interest rate of Iranian capital which had been blocked in US banks for 14 months. In London, Rafsajani said that Iran was ready to protect US oil interests in the region.[43]

The friendship signal from Tehran toward Washington was looked at very seriously, especially during May, when the US government received a series of secret information that was gained from a defeated Russian spy. The US responded positively to friendly glimpses from Khomeini and Rafsanjani, (Speaker of the Parliament).

As a result of access to intelligence reports provided by the US, the Khomeini Regime made the Tudeh party illegal. Two hundred of its member were executed, and 18 Russian diplomats were sent home. The information Washington extended to Tehran, included a list of K.G.B. spies.[44] This list consisted of the highest ranking military Iranian officers. For example, the navy commander-in-chief who, it was later discovered, had given F.14 and Phoenix missile secrets to KGB contacts.[45] The US government was very eager to halt the Russian influence. But the big mistake of the intelligence analysts in Washington was that they took Tehran very seriously regardless of the regime's ideology. Even the explosion in the US Embassy in Beirut on April 18, 1983, by a suicide lorry, an event later claimed by the Islamic Jihad organization, was not taken as a lesson by the US officials in Washington.

Despite the ban on sales of weapons to Iran, over $100 million worth of arms were sold yearly to Iran. These arms sales were usually by American companies and active arms smugglers in the US and elsewhere, especially in South Korea and Israel.[46] The honeymoon between Tehran and Washington didn't last very long. The Khomeini Regime became hopeless about solving its internal problems as well as about deciding the future of the war. The Iranian people were getting tired of anti-American slogans, so the regime had no other choice but to organize a terrorist front, particularly in Lebanon, in order to prove it was indeed anti-American. A few days after the US Embassy explosion in Beirut, the western press reported that Iran was involved. Also, the Israeli information sources said that a fundamentalist Shiite group, under the leadership of Hossein Moussavi, supported by Iran with close ties to Syria, had planned this explosion.[47] It appeared that the Khomeini regime, after executing the KGB spies in Iran, were insisting on their anti-American position to convince Moscow that they were following the policy of "neither east, nor west."

On October 23rd, 1983, a big explosion ripped through the center of the US Navy barracks near Beirut International Airport, killing 241 marines. American experts called, this, the biggest non-nuclear explosion after the Second World War. The FBI said: this was the most successful terrorist attack in Middle East history.[48] On the same day, a similar explosion blew up the French military center in Beirut, killing 88 French parachutists. These kinds of suicide bombings also damaged Israel. One suicide lorry, on November 4, 1983, in Tyre, south Lebanon, killed 67 people in an Israeli military center, 32 being Lebanese POW. The US was taken by surprise.

President Reagan responding to the question as to who was responsible, said he had no idea. Casper Weinberger, Secretary of Defense, said that Iranian terrorists had a direct hand in this mission.[49] Reagan was very cautious about saying who was behind this disasterous explosion and insisted that the US had no plan to evacuate her forces from Lebanon or to give into terrorism and blackmail.[50]

It was apparent that Washington had no clear policy as to how to face terrorism and what to do with the Khomeini Regime.

The New York Times wrote in August 1983, that the US didn't limit Israeli sales of weapons and ammunition to Iran.[51] The reaction of those countries hurt by Iranian terrorist acts was unclear, while all these countries knew that the root of terrorism in the Middle East begins from Tehran. The cooperation between Khomeini and Hafez Assad has added to this factor. In 1983, alone, over one thousand tons of arms and propaganda materials via the embassy of Iran in Syria, reached Lebanon. This embassy has the largest budget in Iranian diplomatic history, standing at over $400 million a year while the number of official diplomatic embassy personnel does not even reach 200.[52] The major purpose of all these resources is Lebanon. No country has really stood against the Khomeini Regime on these matters. The US,apart from accusing Iran of having a hand in international terrorism, did not punish Iran. Only the New Jersey warship with its long range missiles on December 14-15th bombed the Bekaa valley and the villages in the vicinity, which hit innocent civilians. On November 16, French forces attacked the residence of Hossein Mousavi, an old military garrison, but couldn't kill him. It said that news about the impending attack was secretly leaked to Mousavi.[53] The Israelis decided, on November 16th, to send their planes to bomb Mousavi's residence. Sixteen people were killed, mainly women and children.[54] The forces of three countries, France, England and the US, left Lebanon and Khomeini gained a political victory and kept a base in Lebanon. The Syrian army and the Iranian-lead Hezbollah remained as the sole power in Lebanon. Consequently, Khomeini believed that the only effective means against the industrial and military power of the West is terrorism and that Western democracy is defenseless. Thus, terrorism became the major foreign policy of the Khomeini Regime.

At the end of 1983, the Khomeini Regime was unsuccessful in the Gulf war and faced numerous political and economic internal crises. Also, internationally, it was very isolated. The US also failed in Lebanon and was internationally damaged in the pulling-back of its forces from Lebanon. France gave up her traditional policy of permanent support for Lebanon and pulled out her forces. France was waiting to retaliate for the Ayatollah's terrorist attacks in France. Israel was the only country which could tolerate the damage and even gain her aims by supporting Khomeini and selling arms to Iran. Therefore, Israel also gained enormous profit from these arms sales. Iran, in the Muslim and

Arab world, became the most dangerous enemy, even worse than Israel.

1. Benjamin Beit-Hallahmi, *The Israeli Connection.* Pantheon Books, New York, 1987, p. 13
2. Senate Select Committee on Intelligence (from the "Report on Preliminary Inquiry"). January 29, 1987
3. *Washington Post,* May 21, 1982
4. *International Herald Tribune,* May 26, 1982
5. Pierre Pean, *La Menace,* Fayard, Paris, 1987, p. 28
6. Safa Haeri, (private interview with author)
7. Pean, op. cit., p. 30
8. *Iran Azad* (Persian weekly, Paris), January 22, 1983
9. SSIC (Senate Select Committee on Intelligence, Report on Preliminary Inquiry), January 29, 1987
10. Anthony Cordesman, **The Iran-Iraq War and Western Security 1984-1987,** Janes, London, 1978, p. XVI
11. *L'Express,* Paris April 30, 1982 (From report based on "Iran and Persian Gulf Report", by the Center for Middle East Studies, Dallas, May 5, 1982)
12. *Times,* July 25, 1982
13. *International Herald Tribune,* May 29, 1982
14. Jonathan Marshall, Peter Dale Scott and Jane Hunter, *The Iran-Contra Connection,* South End Press, Boston, 1987, pp. 169-170
15. *Le Quotidien de Paris,* June 1, 1982
16. Ibid, June 16, 1982
17. Cordesman, op. cit., p. XVII
18. Annie Laurent and Antoine Basbours, *Geres Secretes Au Liban,* Gallimard, Paris, 1987, p. 248
19. Ze'er Schiff and Ehud Ya'ari, *Israel's Lebanon War,* Unwin, London, 1984, p. 96
20. *Le Matin,* April 19, 1982
21. *Valeurs Actuelles,* Paris, July 19, 1982
22. *Islamic Republic Radio,* June 21, 1982
23. *Newsweek,* June 28, 1982
24. *Daily Telegraph,* London, June 21, 1982
25. Laurent and Basbous, op. cit., pp. 239-241
26. *Islamic Republic Radio,* June 21, 1982
27. *Nouvel Observateur,* June 19, 1982
28. *International Herald Tribune,* July 2, 1982
29. *Le Quotidien de Paris,* August 21-22, 1982

30. *Aerospace Daily,* August 18, 1982
31. *Le Quotidien, op. cit.,* August 21, 1982
32. *New York Times,* March 3, 1982
33. *Observer,* October 29, 1985
34. *World Press Review,* October
35. *West German National Radio,* November 7, 1985
36. *New York Times,* November 1, 1982
37. Cordesman, op. cit., p. XVII
38. *La Libration,* September 29, 1983
39. Marshall et al., op. cit., p. 170
40. *Daily Telegraph,* January 6, 1983
41. *Sunday Times,* January 9, 1983
42. *Le Monde Diplomatique,* July 29, 1983
43. *International Herald Tribune,* February 8, 1983
44. *Washington Post,* January 13, 1987
45. Ehsan Tabari, *Kazhrahe, Khaterati az Tarikh-e Hezbe Tudeh,* Amirkabir, Tehran, 1366, p. 308
46. *Times,* July 25, 1983
47. *Sunday Times,* April 24, 1983
48. Amir Taheri, Holy Terror, Adler and Adler, Bethesda, 1987, p. 134
49. *Washington Post,* October 24, 1983
50. *Le Matin,* October 24, 1983
51. *New York Times,* August 23, 1983
52. Taheri, op. cit., p. 137
53. Pean, op. cit., p. 128
54. Taheri, op. cit., p. 135

8

THE STAGE IS PREPARED FOR IRANGATE

1984 was a very important year for Khomeini. It seemed that his fate and that of the war and the regime could change. Khomeini had succeeded in pushing Iraqi forces out of Iran, and most of the opposition forces such as the Tudeh party and the Mojaheddin had been crushed. He could appoint his own trustworthy people to key positions and shape his regime by bringing socialist consultants from the Eastern block, such as North Korea and East Germany. But, the gradual escalation of internal crises and the disillusionment of the general public did not provide much opportunity for the regime to find proper solutions, except for Khomeini to protect his regime from falling.

The economic crisis, the decrease of oil prices, the cost of the war and lack of victory in the war with Iraq were all strangling the regime. The competition among the clergy, the communists and Mojaheddin Khalgh for access to power meant each would do anything, including bribery or spying to get to the top and help their own cronies, and this struggle was taking a new phase every day. There was also a bitter conflict between the army and the revolutionary pasdars. The Ayatollah's regime had become internationally isolated because it ignored human rights by killing its opposition and torturing political prisoners without trial. Although the regime seemed in control, inside the country nothing moved and everything was in turmoil and highly unsettled.

Some writers and Iranian experts believed that the continuation of Khomeini's regime was dependent upon the special relation between religious tradition of the Shiites in Iran and the charisma of the Ayatollah.[1] In general, this view was not correct because many had believed at the beginning of the revolution that Khomeini's personality was very similar to Ghandi's, which later was shown not to be true. The majority of Iranians, and even Khomeini and his advisors, all knew that the rate of the regime depended on external factors. One was the arms purchases from Israel and other countries with the help of Israel which provided a flood of spare parts and a supply of western goods, particularly US-made. Another was the price of oil. Perhaps, the most important factor was the lack of support from foreign powers for the opposition inside and outside of Iran. When the regime realized that, it could not win the war it started to employ the tactics of war attrition.[2] The purpose was to buy time by extending the war and then, to blame all the economic shortfalls and mismanagement on the war.

The deadlock for reorganization of the economy and the danger from outside, made the regime even more fearful about its future, and as a result of fear hostage-taking in Lebanon, particularly US citizens and bold international terrorism became a landmark in the Khomeini Regime foreign policy.

At this critical moment, Israel again became interested in helping Khomeini to benefit her long-term strategic interests in the region. Khomeini did not know how to take advantage from this moment during which the US did not have a coherent policy of the operational mechanisms of Tel Aviv, Washington, Paris, London, and Bonn. Israeli advice helped the Ayatollah overcome the difficult problems he was facing during 1984 to prolong his own political survival.

Based on various reports by Western intelligence services, it seemed that the CIA and Mossad showed much interest in expanding their contacts for arms sales. But the essential idea was to promote their joint interest in Iran.[3] The direct arms sale connection was continued with Iran via London.[4] But their cooperation networks were more complex and more secret with most of the arms deals being conducted by private middlemen.

In 1984, President Reagan was hurt in his re-election period by the terrorist actions in Lebanon, which showed that the US administration did not have a clear policy toward Iran.

In January 1984, Geoffrey Kemp, the Near East director of National Security Council, in a position paper to Robert MacFarlane recommended that Khomeini's regime was a threat to US interests in the region and that the Reagan administration should consider the possibility of covert operations against Iran very seriously. According to Kemp's report, Khomeini's close cooperation with Syria had put Assad in a powerful position among Arab leaders while at the same time access to oil in the Persian Gulf would be more difficult for the West. The Khomeini regime had both direct and indirect involvement in the terrorist activities against US subjects and interests in the region. Kemp's report reflected exactly the exiled Iranian views, who were his major source of information. The exiled opposition was hopeful that they could bring a government that supports the West with the help of foreign governments. The reports about internal conflicts persuaded Kemp to suggest the policy recommendation which was mentioned previously.[5]

This report was prepared when a few US citizen's were held by Hezbollah in Beirut. During the hostage-taking in Lebanon, Washington was certain that Iran had an active role in putting explosives in the US embassy and the marine base in Beirut (October 1983). Consequently, the United States officially accused Iran of being a supporter of international terrorism and finally, on January 23, 1984, the US banned the export of US-made goods to Iran.

In the National Security Council, Robert MacFarlane was very interested in Iran, while other members of the National Security Council were afraid that Khomeini's successor might further damage US interests in Iran.

As the National Security Council had no clear strategy toward Iran, it was not in position to have any influence over what might occur after the death of Khomeini.[6]

Beside the internal power struggle in Iran and the vacuum after the death of Khomeini, there was another big struggle in Washington about the future of the US-Iran relationship.

On January 20, 1984, the US Secretary of State called Iran a supporter of international terrorism and insisted that all US allies should refuse to sell arms to Iran. However, the Reagan administration was very worried about its relation with Iran, because by the end of March 1984, seven Americans (William Buckley, the Chief of the CIA station in Beirut, and six others) had been kidnapped by Hezbollah, a Shiite organization in Lebanon which is supported by Khomeini. Furthermore, according to various reports, the Soviet Union was in a position to interfere in Iranian affairs after the death of Khomeini. Thus, some members of the Reagan administration were convinced that they should leave the door open for negotiations with Iran in a pragmatic way. US officials thought the delivery of arms to Iran might help gain the release of the hostages and at the same time leave the door open for strategic purposes.[7]

When Buckley was kidnapped, William Casey, the CIA Director, became very worried because Buckley was officially an officer of the US Embassy in Beirut. Casey was certain that Moslem extremists knew what Buckley's position was and he was under great pressure to gain the release of Buckley, because the kidnapping had created great concern amongst the CIA officers throughout the world that the CIA was ready to do anything in order to rescue its agents.[8]

In the summer of 1984, the Iranian officials, in charge of arms purchases, asked some international arms dealers for TOW missiles. The Chief of the Near East division of the CIA told the Tower Commission that CIA operations every year receive between 30-40 requests from Iranians or exiled Iranians who were ready to exchange secret information about important views inside Iran for the purchase of a dozen Bell helicopters or one thousand TOW missiles.[9] At the same time, secretly, two influencial arm dealers tried to create an arms relation between the US and Iran. In political and information circles, it was known that these two individuals had special connectons with Israel and later they were among the important actors of Irangate.

While most of the US government organizations and information agencies lacked any cooperation or coordination about US policy vis a vis Iran, MacFarlane, on August 31, 1984, demanded a joint report of all concerned organizations about US policy towards Iran after Khomeini. Twenty-six US organizations and agencies gave a report about how the US should deal with terrorism but most of the report was based on prevention and retaliation if needed.[10]

On October 19, the State Department, on the basis of Macfarlane's demand, provided a report which said that the US had no influential relation with the Iranian government and no connection with Iranian political groups. This report also failed to suggest how to build a relationship with Iran. Consequently, most of the members of the NSC became disappointed by the lack of results from these reports.[11]

In the joint report, it was suggested that the death of Khomeini was the necessary condition for establishing any relation with Iran and most likely the improvement of the relation. Also, there was an indication in the report that the arms sales to Iran depended on Iran's demands and the official relationship with the US. The balance of power in the region was very much in relation to the volume of arms to Iran, a relationship which needs further study.[12]

When no one in Washington could find any solution for the release of the hostages and the re-establishment of relations with Iran, a meeting between an ex-member of the CIA and two Iranians took place on November 1984 in Hamburg to discuss the situation. This seemed in the beginning a simple incident, but in fact, was a part of a large Israeli-Iranian plan. This was a big trap for the United States and became one of the most complex contemporary historical episodes and an immense political crisis in the modern period of US foreign policy.[13]

Theodore Shakley, ex-CIA, wrote to Washington that during the period from 1st to 21st November, 1984, there was a meeting with General Manouchehr Hashemi, the director of the SAVAK eighth office (counter-intelligence) who introduced Manuchehre Ghorbanifar to him and said he had connections in the high levels of the Iranian government. Shackley wrote that Ghorbanifar was already a SAVAK agent. He suggested the problem of making payoffs to Iranian officials for the release of hostages and said he and other Iranians would like to bring Tehran closer to the West.[14]

According to an intelligence report by the US Senate about Iran which was leaked to the press, the idea of re-establishing relations between the US and Iran was presented in a meeting between David Kimche and Adolon Schwimmer (the Israeli arms dealer who was counselor to Shimon Perez, former Prime Minister of Israel), Jacob Nimrudy and Manuchehr Ghorbanifar during 1984. This group thought the complex part of this plan was the satisfaction of US officials.[15] In other words, the agreement of Khomeini was not a problem. Theodore Shakley wrote about the meeting in Hamburg with Manuchehre Ghorbanifar that they were afraid of Iran, coming under Soviet influence, unless General Hashemi and Ghorbanifar, with the help of Iranian moderates, could develop a constructive dialogue with Washington. According to his statement, the fate of Iran was highly dependent on President Reagan. Ghorbanifar, in order to prove that General Hashemi had good connections and influence, suggested that Iran was ready to exchange some of the Russian-made arms that Iran had captured in the war with Iraq with TOW missiles. He said there is a chance that Iran could be paid cash instead. Then, the hostages in Lebanon, including Buckley, could be released. He assured the Americans, after a few telephone contacts in different places, that the hostages were still alive. But, the conditions for this deal should be through him (Ghorbanifar). Shackley wrote in his report that: "by the 7th of December, 1986, we should respond to Ghorbanifar's request."

Shackley told the Tower Commission in 1987 about the story of selling arms secretly to Iran that the State Department in the end of December, had replied that: "we will solve the problem our way."[16]

Besides this, Shackley sent a copy of his report to General Vernon Walters, who did not respond. It seemed that the activities of the arms dealers and their Israeli partners for selling arms to Iran in order to help moderate groups to reach power did not convince the US officials. But, those US officials were not aware of the secret cooperation between Tel Aviv and Tehran.

The war between Iran and Iraq had become full fledged during 1984. There were no victories but the damage and killing on both sides was immense. In February 1984 Iran, in an attack called "Alfajar," near Mehran, achieved a limited victory. The attack, Alfajar 6, in the Dehloran district, was aimed at taking Basreh. In these attacks, Iran's military gains were greater than Iraq's, but the loss of Iranian lives was enormous. The Iranians used human-wave tactics in the war which consisted of very young men without experience and Basij and pasdar without weapons who were able to cross the well-equipped Iraq forces. The Iraqis did not have enough human resources to face Iran, but they were in a privileged position from the technological and military point of view, especially Air-Force. The Iraqi Air-Force was equipped with Super-Etendard and French-made Exocet missiles which they used against military and naval targets in Iran.

The Iranians, in 1983, got back most of their territory occupied by the Iraqis and during 1984, their defense tactics changed into aggressive tactics. However, they made the same mistakes as the Iraqis did during the Khusestan attacks. Khomeini's forces assumed that because the majority of Basra's population and Southeastern Iraq are Shiite, that they could create an uprising against Saddam Hussein by taking-over those areas. Nevertheless, by the end of March, the loss of Iraqi forces reached 9,000 and the Iranian losses were over 40,000 and the Basra attack had not produced a social uprising. The only major Iranian success in this attack was holding on to Majnoon Island. As a result, the war changed again to a tanker war in the Gulf. Oil exportation from Kharg Island faced tremendous problems. Half of the insurance costs of the oil tankers became a burden on Iran, in addition to a major discount on the price of oil because of Iraqi bombing of Kharg.

At the end of 1984, Iranian religious leaders understood that they could not win the war through religious excitement. Iranian extensive attacks and operations required arms, parts and equipment. Therefore, the two parties were seeking more equipment and weapons. By the end of 1984, both sides realized they were not able to win the war and that the present balance of forces could continue for years to come.[17]

In the meantime, Israel was seeking through its secret relationship with the Khomeini Regime, to establish a link between Washington and Tehran. The American hostages and Iranian arms requirements produced the right formula. The Irangate scandal started.

1. James Bill, *The Eagle and the Lion,* Yale University Press, New Haven, 1988, p. 273
2. Ibid, p. 305
3. Senate Select Committee on Intelligence, January 29th, 1987
4. *Business Week,* December 29, 1986
5. *The Tower Commission Report,* Bantam Books, New York, 1987, p. 104
6. Ibid, p. 20
7. *Tower Commission,* op. cit., p. 18-19
8. Woodward, op. cit., p. 452-453
9. *Tower Commission,* op. cit., p. 106
10. Woodward, op. cit., p. 413
11. The Tower Commission Report, op. cit., p. 20-21
12. The National Security Archive, *The Chronology,* Warner Books, New York, 1987, p. 69
13. Steven Emerson, *Secret Warriors,* G.P. Putnam, New York, 1988
14. Tower Commission, op. cit., p. 24
15. *Washington Post,* January 12, 1987
16. The Tower Commission Report, op. cit., pp. 106-107
17. Anthony Cordesman, *Iran-Iraq War and Western Security 1984-1987,* Jane's, London, 1987, pp. XVIII, 61-67

9

IRANGATE

On the third of November 1986, Al-Shiraa, a weekly magazine in Lebanon, printed a news story about a secret arms sale to Iran by the United States. This news had already been published in a local paper by an Islamic Group in Lebanon. Al-Shiraa reported that a US mission had gone to Tehran and had held discussions with some top officials of Khomeini's regime. This news story was followed with detailed reports about the reasons why the US had sold arms to Iran, the behind-the-scene deal being the release of the US hostages in Beirut. The same day that Islamic Jihad organization released David Jacobsen, the US hostage claimed that "his freedom was in response to an overture from the US government.[1]

On the anniversary of the hostage taking in 1987, Ali-Akbar Hashemi Rafsanjani, the Speaker of the House, gave a talk in front of the ajlis building when he claimed that two days after the Al-Shiraa report there had been an incredible reaction in the US media. These reports seemed unbelievable in the beginning because they contradicted US policy for the exchanging of hostages for arms with the Khomeini Regime. Although the US government denied all the reports, by mid-November all the news about the arms sale were proven true.[2]

Hashemi Rafsanjani, in a speech which was broadcast by RTV on November 4, claimed: "After releasing passengers from the TWA plane in exchange for the Lebanese prisoners who were captured by the Israelis, I had asked the hostage takers to let the plane go. Then, the Japanese Prime Minister on behalf of the United States asked me to facilitate the releasing of the US hostages. Later on Americans began through various channels to beg for the release of US hostages. The channels they used were as follows: UN Mission, different Iranian embassies, neighboring countries and international arms dealers."

While Rafsanjani was talking about the US in a mocking way, he also indicated that they would think USA has a very prudent and wise policy. In the White House, a group of prominent analysts and planners are plotting to deceive the people of the world. Look how miserable the United States is; how our arms sale dealers deceived the US. This should be recorded in history. The rest of Rafsanjani's speech was fabrication in which he wanted to show that the United States wanted to have relations with the Khomeini Regime while the Iranian officials did not want to talk to the US mission in Tehran, and finally they were kicked out from Tehran. But, he did not explain why it took six months until the public was informed.

Nevertheless, the story of the arms deal was true. The US government from August 1985 had entered into a secret arms deal with the Khomeini Regime. US government was hopeful to exchange arms for the release of the US hostages in Beirut.[3]

Our purpose here is not to write the detailed story of Iran Gate or Iran-Contra's affairs (which was the sale of arms to Iran and usage of the profits for the Contra war with Nicaragua). Here, we try to prove that the story of Irangate was a plot that was planned jointly between Israel and the Khomeini Regime. In this plot, the highest officials from both governments, ie: Shimon Perez and Ayatollah Khomeini, organized a joint group of top officials jointly with the arms dealers to achieve what they planned for. In this way, the deception was carried from the President to the National security members and the CIA.

After all, the Ayatollah, the Israeli government and the arms dealers all achieved what they wanted. United States was the only one to fail to achieve the release of the hostages, or the improvement of her relationship with Iran; the increase of US influence in Iran; to stop the influence of Soviet Union in Iran; the increase of her impact on the future of Iranian affairs; and the ending of Iran-Iraq war. The joint research committee of Congress and the Senate findings indicated that "Iranians received exactly the arms they were looking for, but the number of the hostages remains the same; three hostages were released and at the same time, that is during the arms sale, three other US citizens were captured as hostages."[4] The only profit gained by US was an unknown amount of money which was given by a member of the National Security Council to the Contras illegally because US Congress had banned any aid to the Contras.

The Iran-Contra affair became the major scandal of the Reagan administration.[5] The Contra affair had started from early 1985, because the Reagan administration had become very hopeless about the releasing of US hostages in Beirut and then, asked the Israeli government to help US on this matter. Particularly, after the kidnapping of William Buckley on March 1984, the US was ready to employ any possible effort to rescue Mr. Buckley because he knew all the CIA contacts in Beirut. William Casey said after the explosion of the US complex that the rescue of Buckley was very critical and should be resolved as soon as possible.[6]

The sensitive position of the US government in the region, and the personal interest of the US President put the Israeli government in a privileged position. The planners of the strategy to reestablish relations with Iran were gathered around Shimon Perez in order to find a basis for opening the communication channels between the US and Iran. The members of this group were David Kimche, Yaacov Nimrudi, Adolph Schwimmer, Manuchehr Ghorbanifar, and Adnan Khashoggi.[7] MacFarlane from the US National Security Council did not know anything about that group. The supervision of this group was with Shlomo Gazit, the former director of military intelligence, and the president of Ben Gurion University.[8] It is important to know about the background of all the members of the group. David Kimche, a member of the Mossad, during the establishment of the group, was a high official of the Israeli foreign affairs ministry. He was the mastermind behind connecting Iranian moderates with the US. He, in fact, was one of the architects of Israeli arms sale to Iran from 1980.[9] Kimche was able to get the US permission for Israeli arms sales to Iran and he was authorized to sell arms to Iran from 1981.[10]

Yaccob Nimrudi was the Israeli military attache in Iran during the Shah's period. He was an agent of Shovimer in Iran for the arms sale. He also, during Khomeini's period, was in the business of arms sale to Iran. He speaks Farsi very well, he had made the most important arms deal with Iran. Adolph Schwimmer is a US citizen and the founder of Israeli Aeronautics Industry and also an arms sales consultant to Shimon Perez. Macfarlane once said that Schwimmer is an American Jew who has plenty of money.[11] From 1948, Schwimmer was in the business of secret arms deals. He always took advantage of funny companies with the help of various governments.[12]

According to some Israeli sources, Schwimmer was the first person to suggest the formula of exchanging arms for Buckley. Adnan Khashoggi, the wealthy arms dealer, was a Saudi and the partner of Nimrudi. He was a mediator among the moderate Arab countries and Israel. Although a Saudi subject, he was an Israeli agent. He was the man who introduced General Sharon to Jafar Numeiri, the former president of Sudan and helped the Falasha Jews to emigrate from Ethiopia to Israel. Khashoggi's lawyer who lives in London said that the few big arms sales operations to Iran all required Perez's agreement.

Khashoggi provided the credit for the US arms purchases for the Islamic Republic in the Irangate Affair. Manouchehr Ghorbanifar, the Iranian arms dealer, and one of the important actors in Irangate, played a role of mediator between Iran and the US during 1985-86.The CIA and other European intelligence organizations did not trust him and believed he always exaggerated. Despite this, Casey and other top White House officials still decided to use him.[13] William Casey believed Ghorbanifar was without doubt an Israeli intelligence agent.[14] Ghorbanifar was known amongst Israelis, Americans and Iranians. The Israelis knew him well because before the fall of the Shah he worked for the Israeli intelligence service.[15] Until 1979, he was working in a shipping company called Star-line International which was run by Israelis and carried Iranian oil to Israel, and before 1986 when he became involved in Irangate he was actually working for the Israeli intelligence service.[16] The CIA had tested him often with a lie-detector and he always failed. It is said that he tried to exchange information for narcotics.[17] According to a Washington Post report, the CIA believed that Ghorbanifar was connected to the Iranian intelligence agency and to the Israeli secret service. During 1981, he created an imaginative story about sending a group of Libyan terrorists to assassinate President Reagan and sold this story to US officials. Washington Post wrote he had invented this story in order to create a problem for one of Israel's enemy.[18]

Shorbanifar was a trusted man in the Khomeini Regime and he had access to Moussavi, the Prime Minister, and Ayatollah Montazeri.[19] Abol Hassan Banisadr, the previous Iranian president, claimed that he was the husband of Moussavi's aunt.[20] He also was the partner in the Rafsanjani sons' companies in various countries outside Iran.[21] Aghazadeh, the oil minister, was a close relative of Ghorbanifar.[22] Adnan Khashoggi, in an interview with Barbara Walters, introduced Ghorbanifar as the chief of Prime Minister Mousavi's intelligence service.[23] The high officials of the Islamic Republic knew that Ghorbanifar was connected to SAVAK and also was aware that he was connected with exile forces in order to overthrow the Ayatollah. But, this record gave Ghorbanifar a privilege to provide the best service to the Khomeini Regime.

The Boston Sunday Globe on December 14, 1986, wrote that Ghorbanifar introduced himself as a member of the opposition to the Islamic Republic while enjoying a close relationship with the Prime Minister. He played an important role in uncovering the airforce coup plot against Khomeini in 1980 and caused the best airforce generals and officers to be executed. Later, it was said that the central core of the Iranian airforce was wiped out and three months later the Iraqis invaded. After the publicizing of Irangate by Al-Shiraa, Rafsanjani in a speech on November 4th, said that who talked to the US were Iranian security people in the region and one Iranian arms dealer was with them. He said: "This person was not anti-revolutionary but very patriotic and sometimes comes to Iran. I don't know what America might do with him?" After the establishment of an Israeli group, it seems from early 1985 by the recommendation of the Israelis, via Ghorbanifar, another group was formed in Tehran in order to find out a way to access US-made arms. So, Tel Aviv-Tehran representatives jointly executed the plan. Some press reports after Irangate had been made public said that Ayatollah Khomeini had ordered that group to deceive the Israelis and America and even the Soviets but later it became clear that this was a mistaken view in regard to the date of the formation of the Khomeini Regime groups and the Israeli groups. One can easily find out that the Iranian group was formed almost one year after the Israeli group was formed.

On Friday, January 25, 1985, this group held its first meeting in Ayatollah's residence in Jamaran in his presence. Participants in the meeting were Hashemi Rafsanjani, the speaker of the Majles, Mir-Hossein Moussavi, Prime Minister, Mohsen Rafighdust, the Minister of Pasdaram Mohammadi-Reyshari, Minister of Information and Security, Ali-Akbar Velayati, Minister of foreign affairs, Ahmad Khomeini, the son of Ayatollah and the most trusted of Khomeini.[24] In this Jamaran meeting what became the foundation of the oral and written reports of the Israeli agents to the US officials and the disinformation process of the press was established. Various reports of the approaching death of Ayatollah and the war between power-mongers inside Iran were the headlines of Iranian exile press in Europe and the US. A long list of individuals who were moderate inside the Khomeini Regime and who wanted relations with the West was published. In exchange for arms and military information about the war with Iraq, these moderate groups promised the US that they would keep open the borders between Iran and Afghanistan in order to send arms to the Afghan mujahhedin and that they would use their influence to release the US hostages in Beirut. In the same meeting, Mehdi Karubi, an influential mullah and member of the Majles and the director of the Shahid foundation and a trustee of Khomeini, and his brother who was involved the the TWA 847 hijacking, became the connecting agents between Khomeini and the US negotiation team. But, it should be considered that although Khomeini chose Karubi as intermediary, the main actor in the process of this decisions-making was Hashemi Rafsanjani, the architect of the whole plan.[25] When the members of the Ayatollah group began their plan, they were very excited by the way Washington accepted them but they were not aware that Israeli groups had prepared Washington for such a welcome. A few weeks after the first meeting in Jamaran in February 1985, Mir-Hossein Moussavi called Manouchehr Ghorbanifar to Tehran and told him of the plan to renew relations with the US. Mousavi told Ghorbanifar that this plan would succeed if $2.5 billion worth of arms would be purchased. Ghorbanifar, a very shrewed businessman, suggested that Adnan Khashoggi who had a good relation with the Israelis and Americans, should participate in this affair. Mousavi accepted and even suggested to Ghorbanifar that he could use the Iran office in Hamburg for his business activities.[26]

The Israeli plan was ready but needed a very influential person in the US government to convince the Reagan administration to allow the sale of arms via Israel to Iran. This person was selected by the Israelis and was the best person to play a mediating role between Israel and the US. He was Michael Ledeen. From November 1984, Ledeen became a consultant to National Security Council as an expert on terrorism and Middle-East issues, especially Iran. To know Ledeen better, it is enough to refer to this comment by Vernon Walters who said whoever got in touch with Ledeen, should know he was like a plague and more Israeli that the Israelis.[27] Ledeen's wife, Barbara, was the assistant to Stephen Bryan who was working in the Pentagon and had been accused by the FBI in the late 1970s of giving secret information to Israel. Ledeen in 1981, established the Jewish Institute for National Security Affairs in Washington which aimed to defend Israeli interests and to extend the influence of Israeli lobbies in Washington. He used Bryan and Richard Perle, another Pentagon official, in his institute. Perle had a connection with the Israeli arms and industry. A few weeks after the Israeli invasion into Lebanon in 1982, Perle asked Ledeen to go to see the area which Israeli forces had taken over.[28] In this way, the Israelis succeeded to employ all the major actors in the plan for reestablishing military arms and information relations between the US and the Khomeini Regime.

In the previous chapter, we indicated the first contact between Shorbanifar and Theodore Schackley was in West Germany in November 1984. This contact for the first time paved the road for establishing a relationship between Washington and Tehran. During that year, Shackley was a consultant in Stanford Technology Institute which belonged to Albert Hakim, an Iranian-American who used to be Ghorbanifar's partner in arms sales to Iran in the time of the Shah.[29] Ledeen convinced MacFarlane who was the head of the NSC to send Ledeen to Europe to gather information. MacFarlane agreed in January 1985. Later Ledeen suggested to MacFarlane starting relations with Iran and claimed in a meeting in April 1985 with an intelligence officer in Europe that the time was ripe for such action. Ledeen suggested that it would be convenient to make a trip to Israel and hold unofficial discussions with Israeli security about such matters. MacFarlane agreed and in early May, Ledeen went to Israel and discussed making contact with the moderates inside Iran. Ledeen's wife said her husband had an important role in establishing relations with Iran.[30]

According to Ledeen's statement, he had asked Shimon Perez, the Israeli Prime Minister, what was the best way to establish a relation between the US and Iran? Perez in response to the question referred to an Israeli group working on a similar plan. Perez and Shlomo Gazit in the meeting with Ledeen said that Israel was trying to find some connections in Iran. Ledeen also met Ghorbanifar in Jacob Nimrudi's house in the suburbs of

Tel Aviv. In this trip, Schwimmer suggested to Ledeen that Buckley could be released in exchange for arms with Iran.[31] Anyway, Ledeen went to Israel as an official agent of MacFarlane and returned to Washington as a de facto member of the Israeli group. He supported the Israeli proposal about using Ghorbanifar as a middleman for the arms deal with Iran and Ghorbanifar asked the Americans for 500 TOW missiles. If the Americans wanted to reestablish relations with Iran, they had to show goodwill and authorize Israel to deliver the missiles to Iran.[32]

From this point, the important period of NSC policy-making toward Iran began. In Washington, MacFarlane, Oliver North and William Casey supported Ledeen's view and felt that discussion with Iran even to the price of delivering arms in exchange for secret military information was vital. On the other hand, Secretary of State, Schultz, and Secretary of Defense, Wienberger, were totally against this approach. Schultz and Wienberger, were totally against the sale of arms to Iran out of the Iranian picture. John McMahan, the CIA operations deputy director, said in a meeting on December 1985, the origin of the moderates in Iran is a question and asked who are those moderates? He replied: "Most of the moderates were killed during revolution or are in prison."[33]

But, the cowboys of the NSC were in charge of the affair. It seemed most of them even Casey were stuck in the Israeli plot. In the end of the Irangate affairs, when Casey, based on the North suggestion, decided to give the CIA secret information to Iran about the war front and the success of Iraq in the war; McMahan who was the deputy director of CIA for four years and had 34 years services at CIA became upset about Casey for the giving secret information to Iran, decided to resign.[34] The main actors of Irangate realized that from the beginning, it was an Israeli plot.[35] From the start of the plan, some of the government officials were suspicious of the Iranian affairs, ie: Schultz, the Secretary of State, mentioned to Macfarlane about Ledeen's trip to Lisbon that Israeli interest is not necessarily similar to our interest. We also can not rely on the arrangment between the intelligence agencies of the two countries; because it might not let us find out what is going on in Iran." Schultz had expressed his view in a telegram which is in the TOWER's report, he indicated: "I had doubt about the method from the start, I thought if I would not halt this process it would be a great mistake." Macfarlane in response to Schultz wrote: "I would cut every thing." But he did not do any thing.[36]

It was quite interesting; each time Israel delivered arms to Iran the immediate result was a release of a US hostage. But, on February 27, 1986, when US government delivered 1000 TOW missiles to Iran, no hostage was released. During this period, Casey, Poindexter and North were certain that Rafsanjani himself would come to Europe in order to meet Macfarlane. The information about Rafsanjani's trip to Europe was given by North who had recently returned from Hamburg. Casey very much wanted to keep Ghorbanifar and the Israelis out of this affair.[37]

When Israel's group and Ghorbanifar became aware of the meeting between Americans and Rafsanjani. They started to create problems; especially Ghorbanifar who realized there is another channel which has emerged by Rafsanjani. They started to create problems; especially Ghorbanifar who realized there was another channel which had emerged by Rafsanjani's nephew; he was afraid to keep him out of the whole affair.[38] Adnan Khashoggi was afraid to keep him out of the whole affair.[38] Adnan Khashoggi asked for a meeting with Casey. He said that his two Canadian partners, that provided the $10 million credit for the sale of arms to Iran, had not received their money and threatened to publicize every thing. The cricis about the affairs by October 9, 1986, reached to the point that Casey was very afraid. It would be publicized, he told North; "Ghorbanifar, his old connection is very unhappy and any moment might explode."[39] When Al-Shiraa printed the story of Tehran trip, Howard R. Teicher, who was the member of the team that went to Tehran, wrote to Poindexter that the publicity of the news had coincided with the trip of the Iranian delegates to Damascus and the Al-Shiraa magazine always supported Syria. The publicity indicated the struggle about Khomeini's successor. He also could assume that while Casey was worried that the secret talk with Iran might leak to the press, in fact, the Israeli group or the Iranian connection had already given the story to the press. Consequently, this action stopped the relationship between US and Iran without the mediation of Israeli. Referring to Bob Woodward's book, he makes that assumption very certain.

On November 22, after three weeks from the publicity of the story, Casey and Poindexter had lunch together for almost two hours. They talked about the story until North joined them. One of the major topics they discussed was the second channel in the affair. Casey always believed one of the best tactics in covering a story which is in the process of publicity, was by achieving a stunning victory. They, (US) instead of being suspicious of Ghorbanifar, had a direct channel who is Ali Hashemi Bahramani one of the Rafsanjani's nephews and Sam Eli, the chief of pasdaran intelligence in the Prime Minister's office. They had special communication equipment made in Israel by which they sent messages to North. After one week, Bahramani said: he is afraid of sending messages and that his bodyguard would send the necessary messages."[40]

It is now known that after the leaking of the Irangate story in Al-Shiraa that the supporters of Montazeri, ie. Seyed Mehdi Hashemi, the brother of Montazeri's son-in-law, had blown the project. Later on, Seyed Mehdi was arrested and executed by the Khomeini Regime, but it should be remembered that when Ghorbanifar introduced himself to the US, he said: Hossen-Ali Montazeri is one of those channels with whom he had close connection.

1. Reuters, November 3, 1986
2. Report of Congressional Committees Investigating the Iran-Contra Affair, November 1987, Washington, p. XV
3. Ibid
4. Ibid
5. Ibid, p. XVI
6. Johathan Marshall, Peter Dale Scott and Jane Hunter, The Iran-Contra Connection, South End Press, Boston, 1987, p. 174
7. Ibid, p. 176
8. *Tower Commission Report,* Bantam Books, N.Y. 1987, p. 111
9. Times, London, December 1, 1986
10. Scott Armstrong and others, *The Chronology,* Warner Books, N.Y. 1987, p. XVIII
11. Tower Commission, op. cit. p. 526
12. Leonard Slater, *The Pledge,* Simon and Schuster, 1970, p. 223
13. Armstrong, op. cit., p. XVI
14. Bob Woodward, *Veil: The Secret Wars of the CIA 1981-1987,* Pocket Books, 1987, p. 539
15. *Washington Times,* December 3, 1986
16. *Boston Globe,* December 14, 1986 – *LA Times,* December 28, 1986 – Washington Post, February 12, 1987
17. *New York Times,* January 31, 1987

18. Marshall, op. cit., p. 176
19. *Wall Street Journal,* November 13, 1986
20. *Engelabe Islami dar Hejrat,* January 16, 1987
21. Ibid, December 5, 1986
22. Pieree Pean, *La Menace,* Fayard, Paris, 1987, p. 45
23. *International Herald Tribune,* December 8, 1986
24. *US News and World Report,* March 30, 1987
25. Ibid
26. Ibid
27. Pean, op. cit., p. 48
28. *Washington Post,* February 2, 1987 – *Washington Report on Middle East Affairs,* March 1987
29. *New York Times,* January 16, 1987
30. *Chicago Tribune,* November 16, 1986
31. *Miami Herald,* December 7, 1986 – *New York Times,* December 25, 1986 – *Newsweek,* November 17, 1986
32. *New York Times,* January 11 and 17, 1987
33. Woodward, op. cit., p. 492
34. Ibid, p. 507
35. *Tower Commission,* op. cit., p. 487
36. Pean, op. cit., p. 52
37. Woodward, op. cit., p. 505
38. Ibid, p. 544
39. Ibid, p. 558
40. Ibid, p. 575

10

THE REASONS FOR ISRAEL'S SUPPORT OF THE KHOMEINI REGIME AND IRAN'S RECIPROCAL HELP TOWARDS THE JEWISH GOVERNMENT'S OBJECTIVES

The "Iran-Gate", due to the scandal it created and the investigations following it, disclosed the importance and dimensions of the apparently astonishing close relations between Tehran and Jerusalem. But, as we saw in the previous chapters, the mutual Iran/Israeli plan to establish relations and initiate negotiations between the USA and Iran, and to give advanced American arms to Ayatollah Khomeini's Regime, neither began nor ended with this scandal.

After disclosure of the secret incidents of 1985-1986, there was not only no interruption or derangement in the intelligence and arms deals relations between Iran and Israel, but according to different reports, these relations were continued in every respect and even expanded. In 1987, it was revealed that *"some of the Islamic Republic Mullah's have travelled to Israel, secretly, during recent years to negotiate purchase of r arms."*[1] Nowadays, the publications of the opposition groups to Khomeini's Regime, publish reports showing that the cooperation of Israel with Khomeini's Regime, has surpassed the mutual cooperation of Shah's period, to the extent that even Israel has

1979. "Nimroodi" the MOSAD agent, who is now acting as an arms dealer, remembers the time when he informed the Israeli Government that they can gain millions of dollars by selling arms to Khomeini's Regime. *"Some people's eyes shone in Israel. They were laying off people from the defense industries, and this suggestion meant creation of new jobs".*[13]

Israel, officially, denies any role in selling arms, but about 600 private Israeli arms dealers have contracts with that country's Defense Ministry. And they are the ones designated to sell the majority of that country's exports. A lot of these arms dealers live outside Israel, but they obtain the merchandise they sell through their close relations with the Israeli Military Organization from London or New York. On the surface, they work on their own authority, as when, five of them were being prosecuted in New York for their efforts to sell two billion dollars worth of arms to Iran, although they claimed they have been in contact with Israeli Military officials; the Israeli Government denied having had any knowledge about their activities.[14]

It was only after disclosure of "Iran-Gate" Scandal, and the role of Israeli arms dealers in it, that the Israeli Ministry of Defense informed Israeli traders in the beginning of December 1986, that they have to obtain that ministry's approval for any arms deal in any part of the world. But, this is more like a joke, because if the Persian Gulf, and henceforth, Iran's need for arms comes to an end, "The Israeli and South African Military Industry will suffer."[15]

This fact has been confirmed by a lot of Israeli officials. For example, "Mordeshai Vershubsky," an Israeli Cabinet Member from Shinui Party says: *"We shall not sell Arms to everyone; but have no other choice. A drop in our military industry will affect a lot of other branches of our economy. We have no other choice than exporting arms."* It is in this way that the UZI machine-gun becomes the official weapon of Khomeini's Pasdaran Army, after the revolution[16] and Israel has succeeded to achieve her most unpublicized objective by arranging arms deals and semi-secret strategic relations with Ayatollah Khomeini's Regime: safe keeping of the Iranian Jewish Minority, and facilitation of their gradual immigration from Iran with the Khomeini Government's official's consent. *"The Austrian Foreign Minister confirmed in New York that Iran is everyday allowing an increasing number of Iranian Jews to immigrate and leave that country. From July 1983 onwards, 51,000 Iranian Jews have reached Austria via Pakistan."*[18]

If we note that the Israeli arms delivered to Iran in 1983 have been considerable, and the total Jewish community in Iran is around 80,000, then the importance of the Israeli secret diplomacy in saving the Ira-

and sending military consultants. In August 1965, the first training course for the Kurdish "Pish Margah" Guerrillas was conducted by Israeli officers in Kurdistan Mountains. The Kurds provided Israel with a priceless help in the 1967 war, because they attacked the Iraqi Forces and as a result the Iraqi Army was not able to help the other Arab Armies. Israel, instead, after the 1967 war, provided the Kurds with the Russian made arms they had captured from the Egyptian and Syrian Armies. The Jewish Government also gave about 500,000 Dollars per month to the Kurds. Mullah Mostafa Barzani, the leader of the Iraqi rebellious Kurds, visited Israel two times (in September 1967 and September 1973). But, the rebellion of the Iraqi Kurds ended on March 6, 1975, when Iran and Iraq reached agreement and Israel did not find any other way to help the Kurds. But now, Khomeini and his regime have once again started cooperation with and support of the Kurds by giving them financial aid, arms, and sending them reinforcement forces from the Revolutionary Guards, especially in the Northern Frontiers, and in fact have revived the policy of pressuring the Iraqi Government through the rebellion of the Kurds, which is precisely an Israeli policy.

And lastly, the last result of the strategic union between Israel and Khomeini's Regime, is the increasing destabilization of the countries in the region and internal disturbances in most Muslim Countries opposing Israel. This destabilization caused by Iran/Iraq war, has created the impression that Israel is the only country that is internally stable, and therefore, the only American ally in the region.[12]

But, despite the importance of the "strategic" and the "geopolitic" reasons which are usually cited as the most important reasons for the alliance of Tel Aviv and Tehran, there exists another reason in this respect whose importance is at least equivalent to the strategic reasons. This reason which has rarely been discussed, and which has driven the leaders of Israel one after another to sell arms to Iran, is simply "money." Gary Seak, the expert on Iranian Affairs, who served as a member of the National Security Council during the presidency of Ford, Carter, and Reagan, believes that: *"Israel has concluded that selling arms is a nice and very profitable business. One out of every ten Israeli workers is working in the industries related to manufacture of arms. Military products comprise more than one quarter of total Israeli Exports."* Zeev-Scheff, the outstanding Israeli author on defense matters, notes that the Israeli policy in supporting Iran is *"based more on the unsatiable appetite of Israel for financial gain than strategic considerations."* This appetite was increased due to the probability of a lot of workers losing their jobs due to the loss of the Iranian market in *tradicting in the first instance. The first aspect is the confrontation of Israeli soldiers with terrorists sent from Iran. These terrorists are responsible for kidnapping and killing the Israeli Defense Forces (IDF), soldiers who are defending the Northern Borders of Israel against terrorism. In this respect, Israel has no other choice than to crush them completely. I am sure we will succeed in this task because they are operating in a land away from their homeland, and even the local groups in Lebanon are opposed to them. But, the second aspect of the Iranian question is the long range strategic aspect which stems from the geopolitical logic. The objective of our long range policy should not be Ayatollah Khomeini and the group of Mullahs who are presently in power. This policy should try to consider the people of Iran, their sensitivities, their culture, and their history. We should build a bridge to the heart of Iran over the hatred and animosity surrounding us, the Iran that will rise from the ashes of this wild Revolution. Israel should refrain from burning the bridges that exist between her and the people of Iran and should use every opportunity to communicate with Iranians. We should not allow ourselves to be influenced too much by the past or present, and we should not doubt taking any risks in this respect. There are people who say now that Iraq is troubled by this ruthless war and numerous internal problems, we should try to bring about some changes in her policies towards ourselves. But, I do not trust Iraq. We have witnessed Iraq's immoral behavior in the war with Iran. The Iranians are the first people to accept that the destruction of Iraq's Atomic Reactor by the Israeli army has been as beneficial to them as Israel herself. In my opinion, we have more common interests with Iran than Iraq. I want Israel to keep all possible options, even the option of getting closer to Iran".*[10]

Sometime ago, Yitzak Rabin, the Israeli Defense Minister clearly repeated this same viewpoint in a press conference: "Iran is Israel's best friend and we do not intend to change our position in relation to Tehran, because Khomeini's Regime will not last forever".[11]

One of the successes of this policy of "strategic" relations between Israel and the Khomeini Regime can be seen in the Khomeini Regime's support of the Iraqi separatist Kurds. Creating problems for Iraq through provocating rebellion among that country's Kurds has been one of the old objectives of Israel, which was practically cancelled when the Shah of Iran and Saddam Hossein signed the 1975 Treaty of Algiers. But, Khomeini's Regime has granted this old Israeli wish by supporting the Iraqi Kurdistan Democratic Party (KDP).

MOSAD's support for Kurds started in 1958, and Israel provoked the rebellion of the Iraqi Kurds in 1963 by providing arms, ammunition unified front with Iran.[6]

Israel is still keeping her relations with Iran, in spite of the fundamentalist nature of Iran's present regime, due to three important strategic reasons. These important reasons are: maintaining traditional contact with Iranian Armed Forces, keeping the war status with Iraq which has excluded Iraq's Army from the unified Arab armies against Israel, and maintaining and increasing the gap between the Arab World and the Islamic World, which due to the support for Iran by Syria and Libya, and support for Iraq by other Arab Countries, is working towards Israel's benefit.

"Hershfeld," the Israeli Writer, in his book, "Israel's Gulf Option," writes that there are forces within Israel that are interested not only in strengthening Iran, but in strengthening all radical forces in the Middle East, because strengthening radicals will prevent the realization of peace in the region; on the other hand, if moderate forces, such as Jordan and Egypt, who support Iraq, become more powerful, reaching peace in the region will be easier. As a result, the right wing forces are exerting pressure to provide as much arms as possible to Iran.[7]

From these group's view point, the geopolitical laws are constant, while the Iranian Regime and it's internal or external affairs will certainly change. The animosity of Arabs towards Israel will be continued, while, as soon as the present ideological religious obstacles are removed, both parties will once again confirm the mutual interest of Tehran/Jerusalem. *"Israel must keep a foothold in Iran"*[8] *because "Iran is isolated in the world like Israel, and the whole world is opposing it. Iran destabilizes the Arab Camp, and neutralizes Iraq, one of Israel's most powerful and vindictive enemies. This is the fruit born by the Israeli Policy divised in a more logical period. Khomeini's Iran is Israel's secret partner. From the geopolitical laws' stand point, whoever rules Tehran, is somehow a partner of whoever rules Jerusalem. These laws have proven themselves to be true from the days of Cyrus to the present time. We should prepare the ground work for an open, or semi-open relation and be ready for the time when the troublemaker Khomeini disappears. Israel and Iran need each other. It has always been this way and will always remain the same."*[9]

"Uri Lubrani," the highest ranking Israeli Diplomat in Iran before the Revolution, who has lived six years in Iran, and from 1982- the time Israel invaded Lebanon - has served as the Officer in charge of Lebanon's Affairs in the Israeli Cabinet, has best explained the beliefs of those favoring maintaining Israeli/Iranian relations, in a seminar held in Tel Aviv University in December 4, 1986: *"Israel should view the question of Iran from two different angles which may seem con-*

trained Khomeini's Revolutionary Guards, i.e. elements who not only are responsible for the internal oppression of the Iranian Nation, but also have the responsibility for training "The Hizbollah" members in Lebanon.[2]

The "Danish Seaman's Union" has reported that between September 1986 and March 1987, Israel has been the main exporter of arms to Iran. The Israelis have delivered ammunition made in the USA and the People's Republic of China to Iran,[3] and it has even been revealed that Israeli arms have been exported to Iran through Syria.[4]

Though we cited the reasons for Israeli support of Khomeini's Iran in previous chapters, we shall investigate these reasons in more detail here. But, before this, we should note that the Israeli foreign relations are always carried at several levels and it is through investigating these different levels that the logic behind that country's foreign policy can be understood. The first level of Israeli diplomatic relations is: the "official" level which includes diplomatic contacts, official declarations, and manifestos issued within the context of the evident mutual relations with other countries, or within the context of international organizations such as the United Nations. Another level of Israel relations with other countries is: military relations. This level encompasses from encompasses from arms deals, to training of military and intelligence personnel of other countries, and is usually kept secret by the Israeli Government. The third level is: covert operations whose aim is to gather intelligence and gain influence in other countries, and is usually carried out by MOSAD. And lastly, the fourth level includes personal and private operations, which may be interrelated to the other three levels.[5]

On the surface, Israel does not have any official diplomatic relations with the Khomeini Regime and the only diplomatic contact between the two countries is limited to the presence of their respective envoys to the United Nations. But there exists very elaborate relations between the two evidently "opposing" regimes in the other three levels.

The objective of Israel in continuing her relations with the Khomeini Regime, from a strategic point of view, is to continue her "periphery policy" of 1950-1960's devised by Ben Gurion, based on which Israel is to seek some ally outside the circle of her opposing Arab Neighbors. The most important countries who should have friendly relations with Israel according to this policy, are Turkey, Iran and Ethiopia. Evidently, this policy is still valid to Israel, regardless of the changes that have occurred in the political map of the region during the past two decades, and even Khomeini's rise to power and the internal changes in Iran have not discouraged Israel from her big dream of establishing a great nian Jews, who were among the biggest victims of Ayatollah Khomeini's Regime's firing squads, prisons and confiscations in the first years after the revolution- becomes more evident.

Khomeini Regime's reasons for getting closer to Israel.

"La Liberation," published in Paris, in Mid March 1986, reported quoting an Israeli who had recently travelled for business to Tehran (and wanted to remain anonymous): *"Khomeini has given his armed forces a free hand in purchasing arms from Israel and has justified this for his advisors who have been opposed to reestablishing relations with Israel in this way that although Israel is a Satan, at present the circumstances have forced us to sign a contract with the Satan." This Israeli businessman adds: "No one in the ranks of the Iranian Government was ready to accept the responsibility for establishing these relations and carrying out these deals, until eventually, Khomeini himself approved them."*

Even if we do not accept the claims of this unknown Israeli Businessman, still, with a little attention to the process of the evolution of Khomeini Regime's foreign policy in the years following the revolution, and the methods adopted by Ayatollah Khomeini and his officials for establishing relations with different countries of the world, we notice that their policies are incidentally very similar to the Israeli policy.

The Khomeini Regime, also, conducts its foreign policy in (at least) three different and sometimes contradictory levels. The first one is the obvious official level characterized by fiery speeches and continuous threats to "The Enemies of Revolution," and "different Satans." Next is the diplomatic level which in most cases operates on a realistic and pragmatic level. And, at last, is the arms policy which is set and carried out secretly and everything in it is acceptable and justifiable. The Khomeini Regime's diplomacy, contrary to its appearance, has been mostly realistic and pragmatic, if not opportunistic. As a result, the majority of the previous regime's policies have been continued. Getting closer to Turkey and Pakistan, which were considered "Servants of Imperialism" at the beginning of the Revolution, is a result of this realism and pragmatism. Creation of the Tehran-Damascus Axis with Syria, which has a non-religious and laic government and hands stained with blood of thousands of religious fundamentalists and arms deals with Israel, and whose regime is "Zionist-Imperialist," all fit in this realistic approach context.[19]

On the other hand, Khomeini Regime has officially announced that: "Saving the System," *"Providing for the Needs of the System", and "Influencing Outside World" (Exporting the Revolution)* are the three basic elements of it's foreign policy. But, based on its own confession, it has found out that at least saving the system and providing for its needs which are the two basic objectives of Khomeini's regime, are not possible along with ideologic idealism. Is was for this reason that the Khomeini Regime's foreign policy officials, themselves, announced in the summer of 1987 that: *"Every community is forced to accept political realism in order to be able to manage and save itself. This way, the ideal remains constant during the course of years, even centuries, while the actual policy, depending on the circumstances, is always changing what should not be forgotten in the middle, is the necessity of 'keeping the regime alive and safeguarding the country.' But the ultimate objective of this ideal cannot be realized completely under the present circumstances".*[20]

The simple meaning of these relatively complex sentences is that the Khomeini Regime confesses that ends justify means, and to save the system, you must be realistic and pragmatic.

Having relations with Israel, and trying to establish relations with the USA, which was disclosed by "Iran-Gate," though on the surface seems contrary to the religious ideology and even the Constitution of the Islamic Republic, in fact is justified on the basis of this realistic pragmatism.

1. U.S. News and World Report, 30 March 1987
2. The Washington Report on Middle East Affairs, April 1988 (page 6)
3. Ibid
4. Beit-Hallahmi, Benjamin, *The Israeli Connection (Who Israel Arms and Why?),* Pantheon Books, New York, 1987, p. XI
5. *Ibid,* p. VIII
6. *Ibid,* p. 9
7. *Ibid,* p. 15
8. Haareys, 11 June 1984
9. Schweitzer, A. "The Hidden Ally", in Haaretz, 11 June 1984
10. New Outlook, January-February 1987
11. AFP, 28 October 1987
12. The Washington Report on Middle East Affairs, April 1988
13. Marshall, Jonathan, Peter Dale Scott and Jane Hunter, *The Iran-Contra Connection,* South End Press, Boston, 1987, p. 170-171
14. *Business Week,* 29 December 1986
15. *Ibid*
16. Beit-Hallahmi, Benjamin, *The Israeli Connection (Who Israel Arms and Why?),* Pantheon Books, New York, 1987, p. 11
17. Business Week, 29 December 1986

18. An-Nahar, 2 October 1987
19. Djalili, Mohammed Reza, "d'un Iran L'Autre: de la Politique Etrangre de Shah celle de Khomeini", in: L'AFRIQUE ET L'ASIE MODERNE, (No. 140, Printemps 1984)
20. The Journal of Foreign Policy (Institute for Political and International Studies), Vol. 1, n 3, Tehran, July-September 1987, p. 5-8

11

THE ISLAMIC REPUBLIC'S RELATIONS WITH ISRAEL FROM THE USA'S VIEWPOINT

Disclosure of the "Iran-Gate" Scandal was a great blow to Reagan Administration's credibility. Within a period of two years, so many strange and on occasions, unbelieveable incidents had happened and the foreign policy of the biggest and the most powerful country of the world had been formulated with such simple mindedness and executed with such incompetence that the whole ordeal was more like a comic theatrical. Wrong people such as MacFarlane, North, and Teicher acting on the advice of the wrong ally (Israel) at the wrong time (in the Month of Ramazan and when the American policy had changed to supporting Iraq in the war against Iran) had gone to the wrong place (Tehran) to execute a wrong tactical plan[1].

An officer, inexperienced in matters concerning Iran, "Oliver North" and some other members of the National Security Council, who were by far no match for professional MOSAD Agents such as (Camich and Nimroodi) or experienced old Israeli supporters within the American Administration, such as (Fortier, Teicher, Casey) had gotten so preoccupied with their operational details that they paid no attention to the probable damages that the disclosure of their covert operations may cause to the American foreign policy or the American status in the Persian Gulf or the Arab World. "Manoochehr Ghorbanifar," someone who had been tested by the CIA and turned down several times because of lying and fantasizing, was used as the most important contact in these secret operations. Evidently, Ghorbanifar had suggested to North, in the men's room of a Hotel in London, to use the profits from arms sale to Iran for Contras in Nicaragua (in January

1986). North testified that Ghorbanifar has offered him one million dollars in bribes in that men's room.[2]

Meanwhile, the bell boys at Tehran Hilton, where MacFarlane and North had stayed six months before, knew something was cooking. Adnan Khashoggi, the Saudi arms dealer and Ghorbanifar knew it too. These people were considered trustworthy, while the US Senators who are fully aware of all other secrets of the US Government were not trusted and were kept uninformed.[3]

Even, after the disclosure of the ordeal, the President, in his first press conference, did not know whether a TOW missile - thousands of which had been provided to Iran as a defensive weapon - is fired from a tripod or from a soldier's shoulder support.

But, the press reports and the official investigations conducted with regards to the "Iran-Gate" proved that this great scandal was planned from start to finish by Israel and was presented in a convincing form as a diplomatic, intelligence, and anti-terrorist masterpiece. It was Israel who convinced the Reagan Administration in 1985 to down load American arms to Iran in order to gain influence among the Iranian Moderates. The interesting point is that the same Israelis informed the Americans, in the middle of the operations, that they are in fact dealing with the most radical agents of Khomeini's Regime and not the moderates.[4]

During 1985-1986, in order to induce USA to sell arms to Iran and establish secret relations with the Khomeini Regime, Israel, on several occasions, provided US officials with intelligence information about Iran. But, according to the members of the US Congress Investigation Committee, some of this information was false and created false expectations in Washington concerning benefits resulting from establishing relations with Iran. On January 16, 1987, Macfarlane reported to the Foreign Relations Committee of the US Senate, that: *"He has relied too much on the information provided by Israel concerning moderates in Iran."*[5]

The merits of the information provided by Israel to USA in this respect is very well illustrated by this report given by North to John Poindexter, President's National Security Advisor, on January 17, 1987: *"Perez, the Israeli Prime Minister, has sent his advisor on terrorism to us with a special report to brief us on the Israeli plans. With a small help from the USA, it is possible to bring a more moderate government to power in Iran. The Israeli plan is based on this presumption that if the moderate elements in Iran can show that they are defending Iran against Iraq and preventing USSR's influence, they will gain credibility and can seize power in Iran. In order to achieve the strategic objective of bringing a moderate government to power in Iran, Israel is ready to start selling arms unilaterally to pro-Western factions in Iran. They believe in this way they can infiltrate the impenetrable ranks of government in Iran. Israel is sure that the Iranians need arms, military equipment, specialists, and intelligence so much, that providing for these needs can help create long range changes in the inclinations of officials within the government of Iran."*[5]

Nevertheless, a precise definition of the Iranian moderates was never provided. The most famous ones, as revealed by the Tower Commission, US Congress Investigations, and television and radio reports, were Hashemi Rafsanjani and Mir Hossein Moosavi, who are both among the most radical and ruthless officals of Khomeini's dictatorship. Both of them are among the architects of closer Iran-USSR relations, and both favor closed government controlled economy and oppressive anti-human rights policies in internal affairs.

After the disclosure of "Iran-Gate" scandal, the Tower Commission Report emphasized that: *"The Iran initiative has been in direct conflict with the US Government's Policies concerning terrorism, Iran-Iraq war, and (non) provision of military help to Iran."*[7] The Commission members emphasized the point that the ordeal of selling arms to Iran has been astonishingly contrary to the US Government's regulations and traditions. The US foreign policy has been outlined and executed, not by the State Department or the Congress, but "the National Security Council," and a limited number of people outside the government have determined it and a selected group by the council (and without informing some responsible authorities of the CIA, even) have carried it out. In fact, the American Government, contracted not only the execution, but also the institution of her policies with regards to Iran to Israel, and paid the price for it.[8]

In fact, the Israeli Government not only seduced the US Government in accepting the arms deal and negotiating with the Iranian Government, but also enforced her mode of operation and execution on Reagan Administration: i.e. the American Government acted in a way which is the usual trend of the Israeli Government.

Nevertheless, the "Iran-Gate" scandal was only the climax of the Israeli Khomeini Regime's several years old relations which had continued against the foreign policy principles and interests of the United States. From years before the scandal, Israel had relations with the Khomeini Regime and was selling arms to it. In a lot of cases, this policy of Israel had been continued against the US opposition to it. But the US Government never really tried to prevent Israel from selling arms to Iran. Why? One of the reasons is that from Eisenhower's time onwards, no American President has ever really punished Israel for any action she took against US interests. Menakhim Begin bombed the Iraqi Atomic Reactor, invaded Lebanon, annexed Golan Heights to Israel, and expedited the settlement of Jews in the West Bank. Most of these offended the Reagan Administration and caused it to announce it's concern, but due to the military strategy and the influence of the Israel political clout in Congress, Israel has always had the upper hand.[9]

Israel, did not even cooperate in full with the Investigative Committees of the USA concerning "Iran-Gate." The Tower Commission Members wrote in their report: *"The Israeli Government was asked to allow some people to cooperate with the Investigative Committee in whatever way it is more convenient for them. But, they did not accept this. Instead the Israeli Government agreed to answer our written questions. We sent our questions to the Israeli Government, but we have not received any answers yet."*[10]

Therefore, in fact, it can be concluded that the US foreign policy, at least with regards to Iran, has always been a function of Israeli policies.

The members of the Senate and the Congress Investigative Committees, even before concluding their reports, said that they have come to the conclusion that Israel can not be reprimanded for inducing USA into the scandal of arms sale to Iran, because the reponsibility for making the decision was on USA. These members added that: *"The USA cannot let the Iranian ordeal affect her close relation with Israel, because these relations are very important for both countries."*[11]

As a result, the USA has looked upon the policies concerning the Israeli Khomeini Regime relations as a witness who cannot have much of an influence upon its process. And this means giving Israel a free hand in her decisions concerning Iran. The US-Israeli relations are among the most sensitive issues before the Congress. The public support for Israel, especially among the Jewish voters, makes the Congressmen extremely cautious about criticizing Israel. Besides, the powerful Israeli lobby, has always mended the differences between Washington and Jerusalem. Dick Cheney, the Republican member of the US Congress' Investigation Committee on "Iran-Gate" scandal, has explicitly expressed this fact: *"when the relation between the two countries has not been affected due to the issue of Pollard (the Israeli spy captured in America), it can outlast any other ordeal as well, and we have seen this in the Iran-Gate too."*[12]

But, it seems that the biggest lesson Washington learned from "Iran-Gate" scandal is that the American and the Israeli interests are not necessarily always the same, and America cannot always rely solely on the intelligence, policies, and advices of Israel. The signs of learning this lesson can be seen in MacFarlane's address to the seminar: "The USA confronting the uncertain conditions of Middle-East" held in February 1988 in the Geopolitical Studies Center of Dauphine University in Paris, France: *"We cannot expect an anti-revolutionary action by the so-called Iranian moderates. Even if such moderates exist, their number is extremely small and they do not have enough contact with the military to be able to effect any changes in the conditions in Iran."*[13]

1. Bill, James A.; *The Eagle and the Lion (The Tragedy of American-Iranian Relations).* Yale University Press, New Haven, 1988, p. 313
2. *Ibid*, p. 309
3. Woodward, Bob, *Veil: The Secret Wars of the CIA 1981-1987,* Pocket Books, New York, 1987, p. 565
4. San Jose Mercury, 2 February 1987
5. Congressional Quarterly, 31 January 1987
6. Marshall, Jonathan, Peter Dale and Jane Hunter, *The Iran-Contra Connection,* South End Press, Boston, 1987, pp. 182-183
7. *The Tower Commission Report,* Bantam Books, New York, 1987, p. 62
8. Marshall, Jonathan, *Op. Cit.,* p. 186
9. *Ibid,* p. 171
10. *The Tower Commission Report, op.cit.,* p. 186
11. Congressional Quarterly, 31 January 1987
12. *Ibid*
13. *Le Monde, 4 February 1988*

12

CONCLUSION

The previous chapters of the book showed that the Iranian/Israeli relations since the downfall of Mohammed Reza Shah Pahlavi's regime and seizure of power by Ayatollah Khomeini has continued. In fact, after the establishment of the Khomeini regime, both parties came to the conclusion that they have common interests, and their cooperation is a must. As a result of this cooperation, the Ayatollah Khomeini's regime was saved from a military defeat and strengthened the Israeli position vis a vis her Arab neighbors and the Palestinians.

The nine year old relations (1979-1988) have had special qualities of hypocrasy and secrecy. Hypocrisy has been mainly used by Ayatollah Khomeini and his followers who have used the slogan of annihilation of Israel as a means to benefit from the religious feelings of the Iranian masses and to cash in on the so-called "Islamic Solidarity" present in Muslim countries against Israel, especially with regards to the question of the Palestinians. In this respect, they have surpassed and outdone most of the Arab countries, neighbors of Israel, and even Palestinian organizations.

Meanwhile, Israel has never denied her hope and intention for normalizing and enhancing her political and military ties with Iran-regardless of the regime governing it- but has in practice covered up and kept secret her relationships, transactions, contacts, and negotiations.

The secret Israeli relations with the Ayatollah Khomeini's regime has been revealed to the world, after the disclosure of the secret American arms sale and the efforts to free the American hostages in Beirut became known as "Iran-Gate" scandal as a whole.

Contrary to the Israeli claims, both countries were conducting secret contacts. Israel, to achieve her objectives in Iran, has neither considered the Iranian nation's interest nor has taken into consideration her "traditional and historical relations with Iran." She has even, sacrificed the interests of her main ally's (USA) for her own.

Choosing such a hypocritical policy is not unexpected from a dictatorial and terrorist regime such as the Ayatollah Khomeini's. Henceforth, Israel's policy towards the Khomeini regime and the profligate relations between Tehran and Tel Aviv has been greatly criticized in USA, Europe, Iran and even in Israel herself.

Jacques Chirac, the leader of the French R.P.R. Party and the Prime Minister of France (1986-1988), in an interview with Politique International in 1985, in response to Israel's claim that the objective of establishing and continuing her relation with Iran has been to prepare for the period after Khomeini, said: *"I do not believe that at present Israel is helping the Islamic Republic only because she wants to be prepared for the period after Khomeini. I believe Israel is following a natural instinct advising her to help her enemy's enemy. But, in my opinion, this action by Israel is a historical mistake...It will be better for them to worry about the problem of Khomeinism at present than to think about the period after Khomeini."*

Israel did not achieve most of the announced objectives expected from her relations with the Khomeini regime. The fundamentalist regime of Ayatollah Khomeini, due to the military and intelligence help provided by Israel not only did not fall, but was able to sustain Iraqi attacks. The Israelis claimed that "Iranian moderates" are not able to establish a pro-Western government, and do not have enough power within the Iranian ruling class to be able to initiate any significant change. Iran and the USSR were becoming closer. From 1986 onwards, Tehran and Moscow became more attached. "Hashemi Rafsanjani," the leader of the Israeli invented moderates in Iran, announced in June 1985, that: *"We intend to increase and broaden our relations with the USSR."* The future events showed that this announcement by Rafsanjani was aimed at persuading the West to provide the regime with more military and intelligence help. Iraq not only was not defeated by the Israeli arms sold to Iran, but on the contrary is now defending herself more powerfully against Khomeini regime's offensives. In the spring of 1988, Iraq was even able to regain Chalemcheh and Fal, which she had lost to Iran in February 1986, due to the intelligence provided by the USA to the Khomeini regime in the context of the Israeli plan.

The Israeli officials have been talking about "strenthening the Iranian army" and enhancing their "traditional relations," with Iran. However, its sale of arms to the Khomeini regime lead to the weakening of the National Iranian Army as against the ideological army of the Ayatollah, ie., the Pasdaran Army (the Islamic Revolutionary Guards) which was being strengthened, with whom Israel cannot claim to have a traditional relationship!

The Israeli objective to the army of the enemy- Iraq- and, creating disputes among the Arab armies, was not achieved. The continued eight years of war between Iran and Iraq has not only strengthened the Iraqi army, but also all Arab armies, fearing Iran. The bloody war which has been going on between Iran and Iraq has temporarily prevented the Arab countries from creating a unified front against Israel. But, the general feeling is that a cease-fire is inevitable in this war. In case of a cease-fire, the Iraqi regime will be obliged to join other Arab countries, and it may even have to start a new crusade against Israel to reestablish it's credibility. If the Palestinian resistance reaches a stage where "The Arab Brothers" cannot ignore it, and if the Palestinians themselves- a large group of whom live in Saudi Arabia, Kuwait, and other Gulf States- become active, then creation of a new military union (probably including Egypt), will be inevitable.

On the other hand, Israel will face Hizbullah on her northern borders. It is not a secret any more that Israel is responsible for arming Hizbullah in Lebanon. This Israeli policy, however, has been heavily criticized within Israel herself. At present, famous leftist and rightist political figures in Israel are calling the cooperation with Ayatollah Khomeini's regime a big mistake. "Mordechai supplying the arms to Khomeini regime, in hope of weakening Iraq, to arming the Ahmad Jibril faction in the Palestinian Resistence- a group opposing Arafat- with Israeli arms in hope of weakening Arafat." General Aharon Yariv, Director of Jaffa Center for Strategic Studies at Tel Aviv University, says: *"Khomeini's Iran spreads radical fundamentalism in all Arab countries and supports aggressive operations against us in Lebanon. As with regards to the claim that the help given to Iran has been intended to enhance Iranian moderates, I am not so sure such moderates exist in that country. At least, it is sure that such people do not exist in the Iranian government. I am opposed to this idea that everywhere an Arab country is fighting a non-Arab, we should try to help the downfall of the Arab regime. We have lived with Iraqi animosity for 38 years and this has been a peripheral issue for us. The Iraqi government will anyway come out of this war worn out."* Abba Eban, member of the Israeli Labor Party, and the chairman of the Israeli Knesset's Security and International Relations Committee, says: *"It is useless to try to deny this fact that these operations (Arms sale to Iran) have been a complete disaster."*

Moreover, those favoring continued friendly relations with Khomeini's Iran have been heavily attacked in the Knesset's highly disturbed sessions. In December 1987, during the Knesset's discussions over the uprisings in occupied territories, Meir Cohen Avidov said that the provocators are pro-Iranians. Muhammad Watat, the Mapam Minority Party's Rep.- objected strongly and accused the Likud Party of supporting Iran: *"Pro-Iran? Your friend (Isac) Rabin is Pro-Iran. It is him who has said that they are the nation and the country who are friends of Israel. This is not Yassir Arafat who has said this, it is Rabin, Israel's Defense Minister who has said it. Do not forget this. You have a lot of these historical incidents, and should not repeat these mistakes again."*

The Israeli academic community is also one of the basic critics of Israeli government policies vis a vis the Ayatollah Khomeini's regime and the Iran/Iraq war. One of the best comments in this respect was made by Dr. David Menashri, an expert on Middle East, after the disclosure of the "Iran-Gate" scandal: *"The general belief is that, Israel, due to her solitude in the Middle East, will take any course to strengthen herself. But, the question is: is this the best long range alternative to enhance Israel's vital interests? I can understand that the government of the USA agrees to negotiate with Khomeini's regime because Iran is more important than to be neglected by a super power. From the start of the revolution, there have been elements, even within the closest supporters of Khomeini, who prefered the USA over the USSR. But are Israeli interests completely the same as those of the USA? I do not think so. These moderate elements who are willing to negotiate with USA, are they even willing to think about reestablishing relations with Israel? It is difficult for me to comprehend how Israel has hoped to benefit from this ordeal!"*. Menashri, then cites the "Peripheral Theory" devised by David Ben Gurion as the reason for continuation of Israel's mistaken policy towards Iran. The "Periphery Theory" was devised at a time when Israel was completely isolated by her Arab neighbors. However, at present, Israel has a peace treaty with Egypt. Meahwhile, the periphery is much more radical. These factors are enough to illustrate the difference between 1950's and 1980's. In Iran, even under the strictest dictatorship and censorship, the same elements Israel calls moderate, condemn the relation between the Khomeini regime and Israel.

Mahdi Bazargan, the first Prime Minister after the revolution and one of the basic elements in Khomeini's revolution, who is considered by Iranians as a devote Muslim and as one who is well versed in Islamic matters, and at the same time familiar with western life (Bazargan is a university professor and a graduate of French Universities)-

in May 1988, published a long manifesto in Tehran in which he condemned the secret relations between Iran and Israel: *"What is evident and indisputable is that the Eastern and the Western super powers and Israel are benefitting from continuation and expansion of the war and have reached their objectives."* He, then, condemns Khomeini's regime for it's vulgarism and fabrications, and citing the contradiction between the anti-Zionist slogans of the Khomeini regime and it's relationship with Israel. He wrote: *"Among the objectives of victory, there existed other claims such as annihilation of Israel, freedom of Qods and the Palestinians Nation, and saving the oppressed of the world. But, as we witnessed, in practice, by purchasing arms and falling into the trap laid down by Israel, by executing unwise and mistaken policies, we have moved to the opposite direction; the aforementioned objectives have been practically dropped or reduced to mere slogans. The directors and referees of this race for destruction and death, ie., Israel, Russia, and American are happy because whichever party (to the war) that gets killed it is a score for Israel".*

The Future of Iran/Israeli Relations

The "Iran-Gate" scandal, the continued military losses of Iran in 1988 in the war with Iraq, the ever increasing incompetence of the Khomeini regime to manage the affairs of the war successfully, the shake down of the Khomeini regime, the increase in public opposition to Khomeini's dictatorship, increase in international support for Iraq, extreme unrest in Arab populated Israeli occupied lands, support for Palestinian uprising in occupied lands by Arab heads of state in their June 1988 meeting in Algiers, the high rate of increase among the Arab population in Israel, the gradual inclination of Israel and occupied lands' Arabs towards radical Islamic ideologies, the strengthening of Hizbullah in Lebanon, the atmosphere created after the Iran-Gate scandal in USA, the diplomatic and mass pressure and support for solving the Palestinian problem, increased strength of peace movements and internal conflicts within Israel herself; all these factors indicate that Israel and the Khomeini regime will not be able to continue their secret relations in future in the same way they did in the period between 1979 and 1988. The future of Iran is completely vague. Although it is not yet certain when, and how some extreme changes in policies or in government will occur, it is evident that the government of Iran will have to incorporate some definitive changes in its internal and external policies.

Iran is neither an Arab country nor a neighbor of Israel. Therefore, any national or even rational government coming to power in Tehran, will have the right and even the obligation to base its independent national policy on "mutual respect" and "no interference" in internal affairs of other countries. At the same time, the changes in the region, indicate that the period of "natural unity and external mutual interest" between these two countries should be based-like the relationship between all free countries of the world-on the interest and benefits of each one of them. When the interests of Israel and the USA are not necessarily one and the same (and this fact was proven by Iran-Gate scandal), it is natural that the interests and benefits to Iran and Israel cannot always and under all circumstances be the same. Therefore, it will be beneficial to the Israeli and to the Iranian nations, both, to choose mutual respect as the basis of their relations and based upon the recent half a century experience discard petite and short-term benefits for long-term logical and realistic relationships. It is only then that never again "the road to Qods will pass through Karbala" and Iran will not be merely a link in the Israeli Security Periphery Chain.

1. Marshall, Johathan. Peter Dale and Jane Hunter, *The Iran-Contra Connection,* South End Press, Boston, 1987, p. 161
2. Servan Schreiber, Jean-Jacques, "Israel, L'Heure de Choix Decisif" (dans le "Paris Match"), 20 Mai 1988
3. Revue d'Etude Palestiniennes, "Une Sance la Knesset- le 16 Decembre 1987", (N° 27, Printemps 1988), p. 138
4. New Outlook, January-February, 1987
5. Freedom Movement of Iran, "Warning Regarding the Continuation of the Destructive War", An Open Letter to the Leader of the Revolution, Tehran, Ordibeheshet, 1367

13

SELECTED BIBLIOGRAPHY

Abir, Mordechai. *Oil, Power and Politics: Conflict in Arabia, the Red Sea and the Gulf,* London: Frank Cass, 1974

Abrahamian. *Ervand, Iran between Two Revolutions,* Princeton, N.J.: Princeton University Press, 1982

Afkhami, Golam Reza. *The Iranian Revolution: Thanatos on a National Scale,* Washington, D.C.: Middle East Institute, 1895

Akhavi, Shahrough. *Religion and Politics in Contemporary Iran.* Albany, N.Y.: State University of New York Press, 1980

Amirsadeghi, Hossein, and R. Ferrier, eds. *Twentieth Century Iran,* London: Heinemann, 1977

Arfa, Gen. Hasan. *Under Five Shahs,* New York: William Morrow, 1965

Armstrong, Scott, et. al., eds. *The Chronology: The Documented Day-by-Day Account of the Secret Military Assistance to Iran and the Contras,* New York: Warner Books, 1987

Assersohn, Roy. *The Biggest Deal,* London: Methueu, 1982 Avery, Peter. Modern Iran, New York: Praeger, 1965

Ayoob, Mohammad. ed. *The Middle East in World Politics,* London: Croom Halm, 1981

Bakhash, Shaul. *The Reign of the Ayatollahs: Iran and the Islamic Revolution,* New York: Basic Books, 1984

Bani-Sadre, Abolhasan. *L'Esperance Trahie,* Paris: Papyrus, 1982

Bayne, E.A. *Four Ways of Politics,* New York: American University Field Staff, 1965

Beit-Hallahmi, Benjamin. *The Israeli Connection,* New York: Pantheon Books, 1987

Bernard, Cheryl, and Zalmay Khalilzad. *The Government of God: Iran's Islamic Republic,* New York: Columbia University Press, 1984

Bertranm, Christoph, ed. *Third World Conflict and International Security,* London: McMillan, 1982

Berzezinski, Zbigniew. *Power and Principle: Memoirs of the National Security Advisor;* 1977-1982, New York: Farrar, Stras, and Giroux, 1983

Bill, James A. *The Eagle and the Lion: The Tragedy of American-Iranian Relations,* Yale University Press, New Haven, 1988

Brecher, M. *Decisions in Israel's Foreign Policy,* London: Oxford University Press, 1974

Brzoska, Michael and Thomas Ohlson. *Arms Production in the Third World,* London: SIPRI, 1986

Carlsen, Robin Woodsworth. *The Imam and His Islamic Revolution,* New York: Snow Man Press, 1982

Carter, Jimmy. *Keeping Faith: Memoirs of a President,* New York: Bantam Books, 1982

Chubin, Shahram, ed. *Security in the Persian Gulf: The Role of Outside Powers,* London: International Institute for Strategic Studies, 1981

CIA (Central Intelligence Agency). *Israel: Foreign Intelligence and Security Services,* Washington, D.C., March 1979

Clapham, C. *Third World Politics: An Introduction,* London: Croom Helm, 1985

Cordesman, Stephan R. *The Iran-Iraq War and Western Security 1984-1987,* London: June 1987

Cottem, Richard, *Nationalism in Iran,* Pittsburgh, Pa.: University of Pittsburgh Press, 1979

Cottrell, Alvin J. and Michel L. Moodi. *The United States and the Persian Gulf: Past Mistakes, Present Needs,* New York: National Strategy Information Center for Scholars, 1981

De Bock, Walter and Jean-Charles Deniau. *Des Armes pour L'Iran;* Paris: Gallimard, 1988

Economist Intelligence Unit. *The Gulf War: A Survey of Political Issues and Economic Consequences,* London: Economist Publications, 1985

Emerson, Steven. *Secret Warriors,* New York: G.P. Putman's, 1988

Eytan, W. *The First Ten Years: A Diplomatic History of Israel,* London: Weidenfeld and Nicolson, 1985

Fanza, Nazir. *Tehran, Destin de L'Occident,* Paris: Pierre Saurat, 1987

Fischer, Michael M.J. *Iran, From Religious Dispute to Revolution,* Cambridge, Mass.: Harvard University Press, 1980

Forbis, William H. *The Fall of the Peacock Throne,* New York: McGraw-Hill, 1981

Goldon, M. *Shimon Peres: A Biography,* New York: St. Martin's, 1982

Graham, Robert. *The Illusion of Power,* New York: St. Martin's, 1982

Griffith, William E. *The Middle East 1982: Politics, Revolutionary Islam and American Policy?* Cambridge, Mass.: M.I.T. Press, 1982
Grummon, Stephen R. *The Iran-Iraq War: Islam Embattled,* Washington D.C.: Georgetown University, 1982
Gurtov, M. and Maghroori, R. *Roots of Failure: United States Policy in the Third World,* Westport, Conn.: Greenwood, 1984
Hamilton, Lee H. and Daniel K. Inouye. *Report of the Congressional Committees Investigation the Iran-Contra Affair,* Washington, D.C., US Government Printing Office, 1987
Hanks, Robert. *The US Military Presence in the Middle East: Problems and Prospects,* Cambridge, Mass.: Institute for Foreign Policy Analysis, 1982
Heikal, Mohammed, *Iran: The Untold Story,* New York: Pantheon Books, 1981
Heller, Mark, Dov Tamari and Zeeve Eytan. *The Middle East Military Balance,* Tel Aviv: Jaffe Center for Strategic Studies, Tel Aviv University, 1985
Hiro, Dilip. *Iran Under the Ayatollahs,* London: Routladge and Kegan Paul, 1985
Holiday, Fred. *Iran Dictatorship and Development,* New York: Penguin Books, 1979
Hoveyda, Fereydoun. *The Fall of the Shah,* New York: Wyndham Books, 1979
Hunter, Shireen, ed., *Political and Economic Trends in the Middle East,* Boulder Colo.: The Center for Strategic and International Studies/Westview Press, 1985
Imbert, John W. *Iran: At War with History,* Boulder: Westview, 1986
Ismael, Tareg Y. *The Iran-Iraq Conflict,* Toronto: Canadian Institute of International Affairs, 1981
Jacqz, Jane W., ed., *Iran, Past, Present and Future,*New York: Aspen Institute for Humanistic Studies, 1979
Jordan, Hamilton. *Crisis: The Last Year of the Carter Presidency,* New York: G.P. Putnam's Sons, 1982
Jouve, E. *Le Tiers-Monde dans la Vie Internationale,*Paris: Perger-Bevrault, 1983
Keddie, Nikki R. *Roots of Revolution: An Interpretive History of Modern Iran,* New Haven: Yale University Press, 1981
Klare, M.T. *American Arms Supermarket,* Austin: University of Texas Press, 1984
Klieman, A. *Israel Arms Sales: Perspective and Prospects,* Tel-Aviv: Jaffe Center for Strategic Studies, Tel-Aviv University, 1984

Laing, Margaret. The Shah, London: Sidwich and Jackson, 1977
Laurent, Annie, et Antoine Basbous. *Guerres Secretes au Liban,* Paris: Gallimard, 1987
Ledeen, Michael, and William Lewis. *Debacle: The American Failure in Iran,* New York: Vintage, 1982
Lenczowski, George. ed. *Iran Under the Pahlavis,* Stanford, Calif.: Hoover Institution Press, 1978
Marshall, Jonathan, Peter Dale and Jane Hunter. *The Iran-Contra Connection,* Boston: Southend Press, 1987
Martin, Lenore G. *The Unstable Gulf: Threats from Within,* Lexington, Mass., D.C. Heath, 1984
McGhee, George. *Invoy to the Middle World Adventures in Diplomacy,* New York: Harper and Row, 1983
McNaugher, Thomas L. *Arms and Oil: US Military Strategy and the Persian Gulf,* Washington, D.C.: Brookings Institution, 1985
Medzini, M. Reflections on Israel's Asian Policy". In M. Curtis and S.A. Gitelson eds., *Israel and The Third World,* New Brunswick, NJ: Transaction Books, 1976
Middle East Contemporary Survey, New York: Helms and Meier, Various Volumes Mintz, F.P. *The Liberty Lobby and the American Right,* Westport, Conn.: Greenwood, 1985
Mortimer, R.A. *The Third World Coalition in International Politics,* Boulder, Colo.: Westview Press, 1984
Naff, Thomas, ed. *Gulf Security and the Iran-Iraq War,* National Defense University Press, 1985
Nahavandi, Houchang. *Le Grand Mensonge,* Paris: Nouvelles Editions Debresse, 1984
Neuman, Stephanie G. *Military Assistance in Recent Wars: The Dominance of the Superpowers,* New York: Praeger, 1986
North, Oliver L. *Taking the Stand: The Testimony of Lieutenant Colonel Oliver L. North,* New York: Pocket Books, 1987
Novik, Nimrood. *Encounter with Reality: Reagan and the Middle East,* Boulder, Colo.: Westview Press, 1985
Pahlavi, Mohammad Reza. *Answer to History,* New York: Stein and Day, 1980
Parsons, Anthony. *The Pride and the Fall, Iran 1978-* 1979,London: Jonathan Cape, 1984
Pean, Pierre. La Menace, Paris: Fayard, 1987
Perlmutter, A. *Politics and the Military in Israel,* London: Frank Cass, 1987
Perlmutter, A., M. Handel and H. Bar-Joseph. *Two Minutes over*

Baghdad, London: Valentine, Mitchelle, 1982
Pierre, Andrew J. The Global Politics of Arms Sales. Princeton, NJ: Princeton Powel, Jody. *The Other Side of the Story,* New York: William Morrow, 1984
Rabinovich, Itamar, and Jehuda Reinharz, eds. *Israel in the Middle East,* New York: Oxford University Press, 1984
Ramazani, R.K. *Revolutionary Iran, Challenge and Response in the Middle East,* Baltimore: Johns Hopkins Press, 1986
Reich, Bernard. *Quest for Peace,* New Jersey: Transaction Books, 1977
Reppa, R.B., Sr. *Israel and Iran,* New York: Praeger, 1974
Rodinson, M. *Israel and the Arabs,* New York: Penguin, 1982
Rubenberg, C.A. *Israel and the American National Interest,* Urbana: University of Illinois Press, 1986
Rubin, Barry. *Paved with Good Intention: The American Experience and Iran,* New York: Oxford University Press, 1980
Rubinstein, Alven Z. *The Great Game: Rivalry in the Persian Gulf and South Asia,* New York: Praeger, 1983
Saikal, Amin. *The Rise and Fall of the Shah,* Princeton: NJ: Princeton University Press, 1980
Salinger, Pierre. *American Held Hostage: The Secret Negotiations,* Garden City, N.Y.: Doubleday, 1981
Schiff, Ze'er and Ehud Ya'ari. *Israel's Lebanon War,* London: Union Paperbacks, 1984
Segev, S. *The Iranian Triangle,* Tel-Aviv: Maariv, 1981
(in Hebrew)
Semkus, Charles Ismail. *The Fall of the Shah, 1978-1979, US: Author, 1979*
Servan-Schreiber, Jean-Jacques. Le Choix des Juifs,
Paris: Grasset, 1988
Sick, Gary G. *All Fall Down: America's Tragic Encounter with Iran,* New York: Random House, 1985
Stempel, John D. *Inside the Iranian Revolution,*
Bloomington, Ind.: Indiana University, 1981
Steven S. *The Spymaster of Israel,* New York: Macmillan,
1980
Sullivan, William. *Mission to Iran,* New York: W.W.
Norton, 1981
Taheri, Amir. *Holy Terror: Inside the World of Islamic Terrorism, Bethesda, Md.: Adler and Adler, 1987*
Taheri, Amir. The Spirit of Allah: Khomeini and the Islamic Revolution, Bethesda, Md.: Adler and Adler, 1986

Tahir-Kheli, Sharin and Shaheen Ayubi. *The Iran-Iraq War: New Weapons, Old Conflict,* New York: Praeger, 1983

Tower, John, Edmond Muskie, and Brent Scowcroft. *The Tower Commission Report,* New York: Betwam Books/Times Books, 1987

Wells, Samuel F. Jr. and Mark Bruzonski. *Security in the Middle East: Regional Change and Great Power Strategies,* Boulder and London: Westview Press, 1987

Woodward, Bob. Veil: *The Secret Wars of the CIA 1981-1987, New York: Pocket Books, 1987*

Yaniv, Avner. Deterrence Without the Bomb: The Politics of Israeli Strategy, Lexignton, Mass.: D.C. Heath, 1987

Zabih, Sepehr. Iran Since the Revolution, Baltimore: Johns Hopkins University Press, 1982

Persian Sources

Afrasyabi, Bahram, and Saeed Dehghan. *Talegani and History,* Tehran: Niloofar, 1360

Javansheer, F.M. *The Experience of the 28th of Mordad,* Tudeh Party, Tehran, 1359

Khomeini, Ruhallah. *Opinions and Lectures of Imam Khomeini in the First Half of 1360,* Tehran: Noor Press, 1360

Khomeini, Ruhallah. *Imam Khomeini: Collected Correspondance, Lectures, Opinions, Pronouncements,* Tehran: Chapbakhsh Press, 1360

Davani, Ali. *The Iranian Clerical Movement,* XI Vols. Tehran: The Cultural Foundation of Imam Riza, Beeta Ravandi, Morteza. *Social History of Iran, VI Vols. Tehran: Amir Kabir, 1365*

Ruhani, Sayyed Hamid. Imam Khomeini's Movement, II Vols. Tehran: Imam's Verdict Press, 1360

Zarinkoob, Abdulhossein. No East, No West- But Humanity, Tehran: Amir Kabir, 1356

Shifa, Shoja ad-Din. *Crime and Punishment* (Iran: 1357-1365), IV Vols, Paris: Iranshaher, 1365

Madani, Sayyed Jalal ad-Din. *Contemporary Political History of Iran, II Vols. Tehran: The Office of the Islamic Press, 1360*

Mehraban, Rasoul. Perspectives on the Recent History of Iran, West Germany: Ataroad, 1361, p. 211

Hashimi Rafsanjani, Ali Akbar. *Adresses Prologue to the Islamic Consultative Assembly,* Tehran: Public Relations of the Islamic Consultative Assembly, 1362